FROM PAGE TO PLATFORM

HOW TO SUCCEED AS AN AUTHOR SPEAKER

MATTY DALRYMPLE

M.L. RONN

WILLIAM KINGSFIELD PUBLISHERS

Matty dedicates this book to all the event organizers who have given her a platform, to all the audiences who have welcomed her there, and to her virtual author neighbors—Greta Boris, Megan Haskell, Jennifer Hilt, and Jessie Kwak—who have generously shared their knowledge and support on her author and speaker journey.

Michael dedicates this book to Becky Sieve for fostering the spark of public speaking, to his wife Diana and daughter Isabella for supporting him during those times when events take him far from home, and to the event organizers and audience members who have welcomed him around the world, both in-person and virtual.

CONTENTS

Foreword	xi
Introduction	xv
YOUR SPEAKING CAREER	1
Defining Your Goals as a Speaker	1
Creating Your Speaker Strategy	6
What is your speaker mission statement?	8
Establishing Yourself as a True Professional	8
Speaker's Notes	10
THE GOALS OF YOUR TALK	11
What do you want your audience to learn?	11
What do you want your audience to experience?	13
What actions do you want your audience to take?	14
Speaker's Notes	15
TYPES OF TALKS ... NOT JUST THE USUAL SUSPECTS	16
Interviews / Podcasts	16
Panels	25
Workshops	34
Author Readings	35
Keynotes	41
Speaker's Notes	43
FORMATS: IN-PERSON AND VIRTUAL	44
In-person Events	45
Virtual Events	50
Speaker's Notes	53

FINDING THE OPPORTUNITIES	54
Your Author and Speaker Communities	54
Conferences	55
Placement Services	55
Speaker's Notes	58
ASSESSING THE OPPORTUNITIES	59
Consider the Organizer's Goals	60
Consider the Organizer's and Event's Professionalism	61
Consider the Venue	62
Make Your Provisional Decision	63
Speaker's Notes	65
SETTING YOUR FEE AND NEGOTIATING THE OFFER	66
What to Charge	66
If the Offer Doesn't Include Payment	68
If the Offer Does Include Payment	69
Consider Copyright	71
Negotiation Basics	73
Speaker's Notes	75
PREPARING YOUR TALK	76
Slides	76
Notes	90
Handouts	91
Practice, Practice, Practice	93
Speaker's Notes	98
SELLING YOUR BOOKS	99
In-person Events	101
Virtual Events	103
Speaker's Notes	103
THE SPEAKER ON THE ROAD	105
Travel Costs	105
Travel Tips	113
Speaker's Notes	115

DRESSING FOR SUCCESS	116
Match the Level of Formality to the Event and Venue	116
Be Comfortable	117
How about Branded Clothing?	117
Consider a Uniform	118
Best (Dressed) Practices	119
Speaker's Notes	121
BEFORE THE EVENT	123
Block Your Calendar	123
Heed Communications from Organizers	123
Manage Your Materials	124
Research Your Fellow Presenters and Event Attendees	125
Promote the Event as well as the Talk	126
Triple Check Your Website	126
Use the Event App	127
If You Have to Cancel	128
For In-person Events	128
For Virtual Events	131
Speaker's Notes	145
ATTENDING THE EVENT	146
You're Always on Stage	146
Scope Out the Venue	147
Audiovisual Setup	149
Be an Active Participant	152
Use Social Media	153
Manage Your Energy	154
Speaker's Notes	156
THE DAY OF THE PRESENTATION	157
Calm Your Nerves	157
Arrive Early	158
Confirm the Logistics	159
Mingle with the Participants	160

Capture the Moment	161
Speaker's Notes	161
GIVING THE BEST TALK OF YOUR LIFE	163
The Main Event	163
Q&A	165
Dealing with Hecklers	173
Be the Last to the Leave the Room	176
Speaker's Notes	177
AFTER YOUR TALK (IT'S NOT OVER WHEN YOU STEP OFF THE PODIUM)	178
Recharge and Celebrate!	178
Tick off the Tasks	179
Follow up with the Organizers	179
Capitalize on Your Connections	180
Share the Experience	181
Update Your Website	181
Speaker's Notes	182
YOUR SPEAKER TOOLKIT	183
Media Kit	183
Speaker Bios	184
General Topic Information	191
Upcoming and Past Events	192
Event-specific Web Page	192
Headshot	193
Business Cards	202
Demo Reel	206
Speaker's Notes	208
STAYING AT THE CUTTING EDGE OF YOUR NICHE	210
Speaker's Notes	212
Afterword	213
About the Authors	215
Also by Matty Dalrymple	217

FOREWORD

Books have the undeniable power to change lives. The right words at the right time within the hands of the right reader can move hearts, shape minds, and alter the world. I'm sure that as an author you're not only already aware of this special magic, but that you've worked at mastering the art of storytelling when it comes to placing words upon the page.

But what about the ability to transform that same dynamic dance with words to captivate an audience from a speaker's platform?

That's where From *Page to Platform: How to Succeed as an Author Speaker* by Matty Dalrymple and Michael La Ronn (M.L. Ronn) comes in.

The first several times I stood on a stage in front of an audience I was a complete mess. I wasn't only nervously shaking, sweating, and convinced that my legs were going to give out from beneath me at any second, but I also found it necessary to run to the restroom. "Butterflies in my stomach" is too subtle a term. It felt more like a flock of angry Canadian geese flailing around inside. I couldn't effectively speak until I'd

FOREWORD

emptied my stomach just prior to climbing on to the stage to deal with the overwhelming nervousness.

Over the years, though, as I spoke to more and more audiences, the nervousness eventually faded, but the thrill and the rush of storytelling from the stage took as firm a hold of my heart as the idea of public speaking used to take hold of my stomach. There is nothing like the feeling of speaking to a group—whether it's reading a piece of fiction, offering a well-rehearsed keynote, or just speaking openly and from the heart. The magnificence of connecting with and moving an audience is one of the finest majestical moments I've ever experienced.

The book you are about to read captures that journey and more, providing you with all the tips, strategies, and encouragement you need to become a great speaker. I know I wish I'd been able to get my hands on a book like this all those years ago—Matty and Michael would not only have saved me a lot of angst and pain, but they would have reminded me that I wasn't alone.

Matty Dalrymple and Michael La Ronn are the perfect co-authors to guide you on your own writer-to-speaker journey. Matty's transition from corporate seminars to author readings, and her deep dive into podcasting, interviewing, and crafting non-fiction, gives you a clear path to follow. And Michael, with his impressive 100+ books, popular YouTube channel, and commanding and powerful on-stage presence, shows you a way to balance writing, speaking, and an exceptionally busy life.

But *From Page to Platform* is more than just a how-to book. It's like having two experienced and compassionate friends by your side. I've known them both for years and hold a tremendous amount of respect for them as people, as writers, and as advocates for helping other authors with their own success. Matty and Michael not only understand the challenges you'll face—whether it's negotiating with event organizers, creating impactful visuals to go along with your talks, or staying professional in a variety of settings—but they'll do it in a way that eases you through the process. Their advice, sprinkled with personal anecdotes and tales, will resonate whether you're just starting out or already have some experience and are seeking to improve your speaking game.

A key takeaway from this book is the importance of being authentic. In the same way that you likely worked to find your unique author voice, you can find a parallel voice for use on the stage. Matty and Michael will help you with drafting a stage persona that can connect deeply with your audience all while ensuring that you stay true to yourself.

This book covers everything from setting your goals as a speaker to mastering different types of talks. Whether you want to establish your expertise in a particular area, make some extra money, build a community, or simply share your passion, *From Page to Platform* helps you craft a strategy that will fit your personal and professional goals.

If you're new to public speaking, the idea of facing an audience can be scary. After all, it's a far cry from the way most of us writers take comfort in the solitude of stringing words together from behind the safety of a keyboard. But don't worry—this book and these two authors have got you covered. They'll share tips to help you not only prepare and plan, but also offer advice on enhancing your speaker toolkit and continuing to improve. Each section of the book ends with practical exercises to work through as part of helping you set the stage for your own goals and your own success.

As you either start or enhance your path from page to platform, remember that every great speaker had to begin somewhere. Your unique experiences and perspectives are

FOREWORD

your greatest strengths, and you have two of the most genuine and magnificent instructors to guide you along, helping you craft a unique voice to take your passion for storytelling to an entirely new level.

And so, as you turn the page and prepare for Matty and Michael to take you to that next phase on your own journey, I wish you success as an author speaker. May this next chapter in your author life be as rewarding and transformative as the words, stories, and books you've already written.

Mark Leslie Lefebvre
Author of *Wide for the Win* and *A Book in Hand*

INTRODUCTION

Speaking is an art, science, and experiment. The *art* of speaking involves knowing how to work a room and how to make your points as effectively as possible. The *science* of speaking involves managing the details of a speaking engagement, such as working with organizers, creating presentations, and knowing the ins and outs of webinar platforms like Zoom. The *experiment* of speaking is understanding that your field, the strategies that resonate with audience members, and the needs of organizers are always evolving, and you have to evolve along with them.

As an author, you have an advantage over other speakers because you've already mastered two of the most important parts of successful speaking: organizing the story you want to tell your audience and finding the right words to tell it. To excel as a speaker, you'll want to refine other skills, such as negotiation (for when you establish the terms of your engagements with organizers), design (for developing the visuals you use to supplement your words), and professionalism (to ensure that each engagement satisfies organizers and audiences and leads to more opportunities).

INTRODUCTION

From Page to Platform will help you do all that and more. Whether you are a beginning speaker looking to break into your first engagement or an experienced speaker seeking to improve your craft, you've come to the right place.

How This Book Was Born

We—Matty Dalrymple and Michael La Ronn—are both successful authors and in-demand public speakers. We met at the Writer's Digest Annual Conference in New York City and discovered we share a passion for speaking.

One evening, at a New York restaurant and after a day of each presenting several seminars, we got to talking about how we had landed our engagements, the strategies we had each used, and pitfalls we had avoided based on missteps earlier in our speaker careers. At one point, one of us said, "We have enough information here for a book!" The other said, "We do!"

And so *From Page to Platform: How to Succeed as an Author Speaker* was born.

Who We Are

Matty began her experience as a speaker in her corporate life, when she facilitated two-day seminars for new employees about tools and techniques they could use to operate more productively within the company's values. She honed her perspective about what it takes to be an excellent speaker when she coached executives on the stories they would tell at these seminars about how these practices had contributed to their professional and personal successes.

When she began her writing and publishing career, many of her early speaking engagements were part of author readings—an often-overlooked outlet for using a place on the podium to spread the word about your work. Once she launched The Indy Author Podcast and began publishing non-fiction books, she gained the opportunity to share her expertise in the writing craft and the publishing voyage in venues like in-person writers' conferences and virtual webinars.

Her books and the podcast provided evidence of her professional commitment to her topics, helping her secure engagements; each engagement led her audience to her books and podcast; and all the parts of her author business benefited from this virtuous cycle. The speaker's fees she earns provide a valuable addition to her multiple streams of author income.

Michael is the author of over 100 science fiction, fantasy, and self-help books for writers and an internationally acclaimed public speaker. He also runs a popular YouTube channel called "Author Level Up," where he provides advice for writers.

He built his writing and speaking career while raising a family, working full-time as an executive in the insurance industry, and even attending law school classes in the evenings. He perfected his speaking skills alongside many other responsibilities, and he exercises those skills in all areas of his life.

About the Book

As we worked on collecting material for the book between these other commitments, we didn't rely only on our own experiences but tapped into professional colleagues for additional perspectives. Mark Leslie Lefebvre shared his experience with speaker's bureaus. Matty's husband, Wade Walton,

INTRODUCTION

shared his expertise as a video producer to inform our best practices for headshots and video presentation.

We've assembled all that information into what we believe to be the most definitive guide available for authors interested in moving from page to platform.

In this book, we offer guidance on:

- Your Speaking Career
- The Goals of Your Talk
- Types of Talks ... Not Just the Usual Suspects
- Formats: In-Person and Virtual
- Finding the Opportunities
- Assessing the Opportunities
- Setting Your Fee and Negotiating the Offer
- Preparing your Talk
- Selling Your Books
- The Speaker on the Road
- Dressing for Success
- Before the Event
- Attending the Event
- The Day of the Presentation
- Giving the Best Talk of Your Life
- After Your Talk (It's Not Over when You Step off the Podium)
- Your Speaker Toolkit
- Staying at the Cutting Edge of Your Niche

Glossary of Terms

One of the trickiest parts about writing *From Page to Platform* was deciding on the terminology to use.

Common usage suggested that *speaker* was the right word for someone who shares knowledge verbally with a group of people. But what term does one use to describe that experience? *Presentation* not only introduces confusion between the experience and a slide deck, but also paints the role of those people as a passive one. *Speech* is similarly problematic because, although it semantically matches *speaker*, this isn't a book about oratory.

And what is the best term to use to refer to the people with whom you're sharing your knowledge? *Audience*, like *presentation*, paints those people as having a passive role in the exchange, but *participant* isn't quite right either; there are times when the people with whom you are engaging really are just taking in the information you share with them.

Here are the terms we settled on:

- **Speaker** — someone who shares knowledge verbally with a group of people
- **Audience** — the group of people with whom the speaker shares their knowledge
- **Talk** — the specific forum where a speaker shares their knowledge with an audience
- **Presentation** — visual supporting material for a talk (e.g., a slide deck)

So ...

Michael introduced himself to the audience, then began his talk by bringing up the first slide of his presentation.

Other terms we use in the book:

- **Event** — the gathering of which the talk is a part
- **Organizer** — the person or group organizing an event
- **Venue** — the physical location where an event is held

INTRODUCTION

- **Engagement** — the formal agreement a speaker has with an event organizer to give a talk

So ...

Matty accepted an engagement for a talk about podcasting for authors at the New England Crime Bake event, which was hosted by Sisters in Crime New England and whose venue was the Dedham Hilton.

Finally, we distinguish between **podium** and **lectern**—a podium is the raised stage from which speakers deliver their talks, while a lectern is the stand, usually with a slanted top, on which speakers might rest their notes.

Speaker's Notes

At the end of each section, we include questions for you to answer. How does the information we've shared resonate with you as you consider your transition from page to platform? What actions will you commit to take based on what you've learned?

You can capture your responses in the downloadable document available at https://www.theindyauthor.com/from-page-to-platform.html. These Speaker's Notes will serve as a map for your transition from page to platform, enabling you to track your progress and adjust course as needed.

YOUR SPEAKING CAREER

The first step in paving the way to your transition from page to platform is to be clear about what your goals are. Once you have a clear understanding of your goals, you can define criteria against which to assess opportunities and craft a speaker mission statement to achieve it.

Defining Your Goals as a Speaker

As with any journey, you vastly improve your chances of reaching your desired destination if you understand what your goals are before you embark. In this section, we review some of the most common goals of authors looking to move from page to platform. As you read through these, note which feel most aligned to what you want from your speaker career.

- Establishing expertise
- Earning direct income
- Earning indirect income
- Building community
- Learning

- Traveling
- Paying it forward

Establishing Expertise

Especially for non-fiction authors, using a speaking career to establish expertise is a common goal. As an author, you have instant credibility—you've invested the time and effort to capture your knowledge about a topic, to commit it to paper, and to see it through the publishing process, whether indie or traditional. For fiction authors, speaking engagements offer the opportunity to demonstrate your expertise in the writing process or in the world you've created in your books. So many people dream of writing and publishing a book but never do; the fact that you have done so commands immediate respect from an audience and establishes you as a subject matter expert.

By expanding your professional platform from author to speaker, you will expand your ability to share your expertise with audiences. As your speaker reputation grows, you will become a go-to resource for event organizers. The more you speak, the more you demonstrate your expertise, and the process becomes self-reinforcing.

Earning Direct Income

We believe that professional speakers deserve financial compensation for their efforts, and earning direct income from your speaking engagements is a goal well within reach.

Paid speaking engagements are a great additional stream of income to add to your book royalties. In fact, Matty has earned more from her speaking engagements about podcasting for authors than she has from her book *The Indy Author's Guide to Podcasting for Authors*. Those are engagements she might not have landed if she hadn't been able to reference the book as evidence of her study of the topic. For

Michael, each paid engagement supports not only his goal of direct income as an author speaker but also his ability to request and receive higher fees for subsequent talks.

You will certainly encounter organizers who believe that any speaking engagement should be accepted "for exposure." These people don't understand the economic realities of speaking as a profession, and it's useful to have a ready response for when they approach you with a request for a pro bono engagement, or if they question your intention to earn income from your speaking work. For example, Matty explains that she supports writers with free resources via TheIndyAuthor.com, The Indy Author Podcast, and The Indy Author YouTube channel.

Although you may make exceptions to your decision to earn direct income as a speaker—for example, you might agree to speak at your local library for no fee—these should be well-considered circumstances, not ones forced upon you by people who don't understand the realities of a professional speaking career.

Earning Indirect Income

Although you should never allow yourself to be pressured into accepting a pro bono speaking engagement if your goal is to earn direct income, sometimes exposure is exactly what you need to maximize your opportunities for earning indirect income.

Just as being an author can provide a path to speaking engagements, speaking engagements can provide a path to sales of other products or services that have income potential. For example, you might accept unpaid engagements in exchange for being able to sell your book to event attendees.

Sometimes the route to indirect income is not as immediate as book sales at an event; merely establishing your authority on a topic can have financial benefits. Perhaps a robust résumé as a speaker will qualify you for a desired job or business relationship. For Matty, landing speaking engagements on topics that appeal to authors is helpful when approaching author service companies as possible sponsors of The Indy Author Podcast. Michael has received many paid invitations to speak because of the exposure provided by unpaid talks.

You can maximize the potential for indirect income by accepting engagements where organizers will make a recording of your talk available to people who didn't attend the event, since you and your message will reach a wider audience, often long after the actual event is done. If the organizers are not recording your talk, ask if you can record it and post it on your website and social media. In fact, organizers may be more willing to agree to this if they are not paying you for your talk, since it is a way of compensating you for your time and effort.

Distributing your talk's content online in as many ways as possible will increase your short- and long-term discoverability, which will lead to indirect income. As a bonus, you'll widen the pool of organizers who will consider your pitch if you are willing to do it for free.

Building Community

Speaking engagements introduce you to a community that, by definition, shares an interest in your areas of expertise. If you match your topic appropriately to your audience, and if you deliver an outstanding talk, you'll build your community of followers and fans.

You can build community with colleagues as well, especially with in-person events. Some of the best connections often start with a casual conversation by the coffee urns or in an event banquet room when you're seated next to someone you're meeting for the first time. As a speaker, you'll be forming connections with organizers and fellow speakers as well as attendees, enabling you to build both your influence and your tribe.

And while in-person interactions can be powerful, virtual interactions are also valuable. You can reach more people in a virtual space than you can in a hotel conference room, so virtual speaking engagements are a great way to build your influence and community.

Learning

A speaking career is not only an opportunity to share your expertise with others; it's also a great way to increase your own knowledge. Organizers often allow speakers to attend other event talks at no charge. And not only can you learn from those talks, but you may also have a chance to interact with those experts and learn from them one-on-one.

Matty has drawn many of her expert guests for The Indy Author Podcast from among people she has met at her speaking engagements, and those conversations enable her to deepen her learning even further (and to share it with her fellow authors).

A focus on learning doesn't preclude other benefits. Michael once received an invitation to speak at an event where the organizers paid for his hotel but not the travel. He reviewed the speaker list and identified a few authors he wanted to meet. He ended up having dinner with an author who showed him the ins and outs of Facebook ads, and the revenue Michael made in the next month paid for the travel costs he incurred—a nice combination of learning and indirect income!

Even the venue itself can provide a learning opportunity. Michael traveled to Saudi Arabia to speak about indie publishing at an international book fair where 600 publishers from 50 countries gathered. Michael took the event as an opportunity to learn about indie publishing and reader preferences in a growing market that few in the West understand. He got to meet speculative fiction publishers and authors in the region, gaining insights that could help him sell more of his own novels in that market.

Traveling

Michael's opportunity to speak at the book fair in Saudi Arabia highlights an underrated perk of a speaking career: the opportunity to travel. You may be invited to a city or country you've always wanted to visit, and the speaking gig provides you the opportunity. It might even finance the trip!

Travel exposes you to new people, new cultures, and new ideas that may become inspirations for new talks or even new books.

Paying it Forward

Perhaps your goal is to pay it forward. Your life might have been changed for the better when you heard someone speak on a topic, and you want to pay it forward by offering that opportunity to others.

Creating Your Speaker Strategy

There are as many variations and combinations of goals for a speaking career as there are speakers, and as you read through the list of opportunities above, you may find them all appealing. However, it's important to have a strategy for your speaking career that ensures you direct your energies appropriately and apply the tactics that will help you achieve your highest priority goals.

What are the top three goals for your speaking career?

Michael's top three goals are to:

- sharpen his speaking skills

- grow his influence in the publishing industry
- continue learning

Matty's top three goals are to:

- build her community of fellow authors and indie publishers
- establish and share her expertise in writing and publishing-related topics
- earn direct and indirect income from speaking engagements

Consider what your top three goals are; you'll have a chance to capture them at the end of this section.

Perhaps you're embarking on this book with no clearly defined goal for a speaking career. If that's the case, try reverse-engineering your goals. As you research opportunities, consider what makes you gravitate to one opportunity and bypass another. Maybe major in-person events or popular virtual events that attract large audiences seem appealing, which might suggest that exposure to establish expertise is a primary driver. Maybe you prefer more intimate venues, especially smaller in-person events, which might suggest that community-building is a primary driver. Consider what's driving your preferences and what that might imply about what you hope to gain from those experiences.

What criteria will you use to assess a speaking opportunity?

As your goals come into focus, craft a question to ask yourself to help assess each opportunity.

Michael's question is, "Can I learn something or meet someone influential, and use that experience to strengthen my expertise?"

Matty's question is, "Will the time, effort, and money I expend on this speaking engagement compensate me in terms of my top three goals (building community, establishing and sharing expertise, and earning income)?"

What are *your* criteria?

What is your speaker mission statement?

You may approach your author career with a speaker mission statement in mind, but it's much more common for that mission statement to emerge as you solidify and prioritize your goals and understand what criteria you will use to assess the opportunities. When you have a solid foundation of goals and criteria, you should be able to craft a one-sentence mission statement for your speaking career.

Michael's mission statement is, "To establish myself as an international expert on all topics related to writing and publishing, and to be among the world's best public speakers so that I can always be in demand. Being continuously in demand leads to more speaking opportunities, which leads to more knowledge and connections."

Matty's mission statement is, "To expand my community of fellow authors and publishers, to reach those who can benefit from my expertise, and to add direct and indirect income from my speaking engagements to my multiple streams of author income."

What is the mission statement for *your* speaking career?

Establishing Yourself as a True Professional

There is one more aspect that is key to a successful speaking career, and that is establishing yourself as a true professional. If you take one message from this book, it is that *profession-*

alism is everything. Every other aspect of a successful transition from page to platform flows from that.

Professionalism means knowing your topic inside out. Professionalism means having effective speaking skills, a speaker toolkit (including a quality website), and high-quality presentations. Professionalism means refining your talk so that the audience assumes you've shared your message dozens of times, even if it's your first time. Professionalism means delivering to the same standard of excellence for a half-dozen attendees as for a thousand.

True professionalism isn't tied to tenure; it's tied to behavior. Event organizers, your audience, and your writing and publishing colleagues are subconsciously (or consciously) assessing your level of professionalism in every interaction they have with you. That applies whether you're proposing yourself as a speaker, negotiating your compensation, greeting audience members as they enter the venue, answering their questions thoughtfully (even if the questions seem silly), or acknowledging fellow event attendees as you pass them in the hallways. Every encounter you have is an interview for an opportunity you might not even be aware of.

Your priority as a professional speaker must be to make the interactions you have with all these people rewarding and enjoyable for all involved.

Professionalism means being reasonable and easy to work with. Event organizers are busy people, and they will appreciate speakers who make their lives easier. Aim to be the speaker who makes organizers smile when they think of you after the event. Giving them that experience of professionalism will increase the chances they will think of you for a future event. It may even encourage the organizer to share their experience with their friends and colleagues, which will lead to more engagements for you.

Professionalism also means being a pleasant person to be around for event attendees and fellow speakers. You don't want to be "that" speaker that people mutter about under their breath when they recall the event because you elbowed your way to the bar or scoffed at questions.

Speakers who behave like prima donnas don't win fans and followers, don't develop valuable creative and business communities, and don't get repeat invitations from the organizers.

Professionalism is everything—a theme we will return to throughout this book.

What does professionalism mean to you?

Speaker's Notes

Capture your responses to the questions below in the downloadable document available at https://www.theindyauthor.com/from-page-to-platform.html.

- What are your top three goals for your speaking career, in priority order?
- If you haven't yet identified your top goals, what type of speaking engagements do you find most appealing, and why? What might this imply about your underlying goals?
- What question will you ask yourself to assess opportunities?
- What is your speaker mission statement?
- What are three keys to professionalism that you will commit to demonstrate in all your speaker interactions?

THE GOALS OF YOUR TALK

Once you've determined your goals for your speaking career, you need to consider the goal of the talks you will give. To lay the groundwork for a professional and successful talk, consider these questions:

- What do you want your audience to learn?
- What do you want your audience to experience?
- What actions do you want the audience to take?

Your answers to these questions will determine both the content of your talk and the approach you take.

What do you want your audience to learn?

This is the easiest of the three questions to answer. You have landed a gig as a speaker because you have expert information to share on a topic, and that information—or a subset of it—is what you want the audience to learn.

We'll explore the best practices regarding choosing your content in the section on "Preparing Your Talk," but here it's enough to say that covering the information implied by the title of your talk is necessary but not sufficient; each talk should include a few "golden nuggets" that the audience can get only from you.

For Michael, golden nuggets are pieces of information that are worth the cost of admission. Examples of Michael's golden nuggets include:

- Information that the average person would never know about the topic that makes them say, "Wow!"
- Information that saves the audience members money, time, or effort
- Information that provides audience members with a strategic advantage

In Michael's opinion, the best golden nuggets are ones that your audience members can act on easily, with little time and money spent.

Matty uncovers valuable nuggets to share with her audience by integrating nautical metaphors into discussions about the writing craft and the publishing voyage. For instance, she may use the phrase "a rising tide raises all boats" to emphasize the significance of fostering an abundance mindset within one's author community or employ the concept of a sailor's "short tack" to highlight opportunities presented by short fiction.

These nuggets can form the foundation for the content you provide; keeping them always front-of-mind will keep your presentation focused and on point.

The information you share doesn't necessarily need to be groundbreaking, but the way you present it should be. In Michael's talks on productivity for writers, he explains the virtues of "writing in the cracks of life," and how he finds time to write on his phone when other people are doom-scrolling on a news site or watching cat videos on YouTube. In Matty's talks about podcasting for authors, she uses the analogy of a publishing aggregator like Draft2Digital, which many members of the audience will know and understand, to explain the function of a podcast distribution platform like Libsyn.

Also consider that your audience will expect you not only to be expert in your own work and perspective, but also to be current in what is going on in your topic area in general. You need to stay on top of developments in your field and have your finger on the pulse of what is going on in your niche. No one wants to hear a speaker who specializes in how things were done ten years ago. Audiences want to know what's coming next.

What do you want your audience to experience?

Providing valuable information to your audience is a requirement of a good presentation, but ideally you will give them more than that. You want to provide them with something that stays with them after they leave the banquet hall or after they log out of the virtual meeting space. This means giving them not just facts, but an experience.

Maybe this means encouraging your audience to **get out of their seats**. If you're speaking to authors who have spent a day sitting in the event meeting rooms, lead them in a stretch that they can use when they get home to their writing desks as well.

A **giveaway** can provide an experience for your audience. Michael often gives away one of his books to participants as a thank you for attending the talk. He doesn't impose any requirements, such as signing up for an email list, to redeem the giveaway. He earns goodwill from participants, and he sets himself apart from many of his fellow speakers with this "no strings attached" offering. Removing barriers builds trust, and participants are likely to become true fans. And although it may seem counterintuitive to provide content for free, especially if you have a primary goal of earning income, giveaways can lead new fans to your other, for-purchase content.

Factor in the size of your portfolio when deciding whether to offer a giveaway of one of your books. Michael has written more than 100 books, so he can afford to give some away with little financial impact. If you have a smaller portfolio, some other giveaway might be more effective; consider offering a checklist or attendee-exclusive video or interview. When Matty gives talks on indie publishing, she offers attendees a special summary graphic that illustrates the various aspects of the indie publishing process. Your options are limited only by your imagination!

The **Q&A** is another great way to elevate your talk to an experience, since it gives audience members a chance to explore how the information you've shared applies to their own lives.

We've incorporated the concept of experience in the "Speaker's Notes" sections at the end of each section, encouraging you to take an active role as you absorb the information in this book.

What actions do you want your audience to take?

If your audience listens attentively to your talk and claps politely at the end but never acts on the knowledge and insights you've shared, you haven't provided value to them as a speaker.

Give them opportunities to consider your talk not just in the abstract but also as it applies to them specifically. Asking them to document a plan and to commit to executing that plan encourages them to take action. Depending on the venue and the topic, you could even pair up participants at the end of your talk to give them a chance to discuss their plans with someone else. This has the added benefit of enabling them to tap into the knowledge and perspectives of their discussion partners.

The "Speaker's Notes" at the end of each section of this book is an example of encouraging an audience to act on what they've learned. By asking you to consider how the information we've shared applies to your own situation and to document your answers to these questions, we pave the way for you to take action on your insights.

Once you understand the goals of your talk and your goals for your speaker career, you can effectively match these to the types of speaking engagements you consider pursuing.

Speaker's Notes

Capture your responses to the questions below in the downloadable document available at https://www.theindyauthor.com/from-page-to-platform.html.

- What do you want your audience to learn?
- What do you want your audience to experience?
- What actions do you want your audience to take?

TYPES OF TALKS ... NOT JUST THE USUAL SUSPECTS

When you think about your speaking career, you may have in mind the experience of sharing your expertise with an audience in a presentation format. These are the most common type of talks, and we delve into those in detail in the section on "Preparing Your Talk."

In this section, we review the experience, the medium, and the benefits of some of the other types of engagements you may encounter in your speaker career:

- Interviews / podcasts
- Panels
- Workshops
- Author readings
- Keynotes

Interviews / Podcasts

Participating in interviews as the interviewee taps into the same skills and can produce the same benefits as other speaking engagements. These interviews might take place in person at an event, be broadcast live on a streaming service or via a local radio or television station, or be recorded. One of the most popular formats—either live or recorded—is the podcast format.

We are both believers in the power of podcasting. Matty hosts The Indy Author Podcast, where she interviews guest experts on topics related to the writing craft and the publishing voyage. She is also the author of *The Indy Author's Guide to Podcasting for Authors: Creating Connections, Community, and Income*, the definitive book on this topic. Michael has hosted several podcasts and has been a guest on dozens more.

The best practices for podcasts are largely the same as the best practices for other interview formats, and since we both have extensive experience with podcasts, we frame our discussion of interviews in that context and note where different venues require different approaches.

Assessing the Options

One advantage podcast interviews have over other types of speaking engagements is that you can easily check out the various options before you choose which to pursue and decide how best to position yourself. The best interviewees are enthusiastic interview listeners, and they understand the expectations of the host and the audience.

For podcasts specifically, there's no excuse for pitching yourself to a podcast before listening to at least one and preferably several of the episodes. If you're asking a host to spend several hours prepping for, conducting, and producing your interview, then you owe it to them to familiarize yourself with their podcast. (If you're really crunched for time, listen to the episodes at double speed.)

Consider the Experience

Another benefit of familiarizing yourself with the pool of

possible interview opportunities is that you can prioritize those that feel most personally compatible; this can be especially helpful for your first experiences as an interviewee. If you're an introvert, you can prioritize interviewers with a calmer gestalt. If you're high energy, you can look for interviewers who will match that energy.

Another factor to consider is the host-and-guest structure. Non-podcast interviews generally have one host and one guest, whereas podcasts can have multiple hosts interviewing one guest, or one host interviewing multiple guests. Acquaint yourself with the dynamics of the different approaches and decide what type you'll prioritize. Matty would never turn down an interview based solely on the host-and-guest structure. However, as an interviewee, she prefers the flow of one-on-one interactions, and when making decisions about interview opportunities to pursue, she prioritizes these. (If you're on a panel of guests, review the best practices in the section on "Panels.")

Regardless of the interviewer's style or the interview structure, you'll be expected to engage in an interactive conversation on your topic, not deliver a monologue or a sales pitch. Pay attention to the questions the interviewer asks you and respond to them; don't walk through some preprogrammed list of facts you want to share. The experience will be better for you and your host and far better for your audience.

Consider the Medium

Another consideration is the medium—e.g., whether it is audio-only or audio and video, how much post-production editing will be done, and whether the interview will be prerecorded or live.

You don't want to show up in your bathrobe for what you think is an audio-only interview to find that the host expects to record video as well. In fact, there's no harm in treating every engagement as if video will be broadcast. The extra effort you put into creating a professional appearance for yourself and your background can translate into a more professional performance.

You can usually get a sense of how much post-production editing an interviewer will do by listening to backlist interviews or podcast episodes. If you don't hear many pauses or *uh*s or *um*s, the interview was probably edited. If you hear more verbal tics or overt flubs, the interviewer probably plans to air your interview as recorded.

Knowing whether an interview will be prerecorded or broadcast live has less to do with your prep and more to do with how you handle the interview itself. For example, you won't be able to ask to restate an answer to a question. (In general, you should avoid doing this even for prerecorded interviews, because it will cause more work for your interviewer to edit out your initial response.) You may have to begin your interview at a specific time and have less flexibility in asking questions of your interviewer or building rapport before the interview begins.

Consider the Benefits

As with recorded presentations, interviews—especially podcast interviews—live on indefinitely online, supporting your speaker goals and delivering your prioritized benefits long after the *Record* light goes off.

Note, though, that direct income is *not* a common benefit of interviews. Matty has hosted many guests on The Indy Author Podcast who command speaker fees of thousands of dollars, but none has ever asked for payment. However, although interviews are typically done pro bono, you often have the opportunity to pitch your products or services, usually at the end of the interview, thereby leading to indirect income.

Preparing the Pitch

Only pitch platforms or podcasts that address your niche. Matty sometimes receives pitches from authors who have written their first book and want to come on The Indy Author Podcast to discuss it; their pitches would be more appropriate for book tour-type podcasts. Don't get on an interviewer's "no fly" list by proposing a topic that doesn't make sense for them; you might have the perfect topic for them at another time, and you'll want to approach them with a clean record as a potential interviewee.

Tap into the research you've done to tailor your pitch. Reflect your familiarity with the program and host; Matty is a sucker for any pitch that includes a reference to her beloved nautical metaphors for the writing craft and the publishing voyage.

Keep your pitch mail short—aim for half a dozen sentences. Explain who you are, what you have written, and why your topic would be a good fit for the host's audience. Perhaps reference other episodes for which your topic would be a good companion piece. Your pitch will be much more successful if it demonstrates that you have listened to the show and provides a compelling reason why the audience would be interested in you and your message.

Provide links to supporting material such as other interviews you have done as well as to your website and social media accounts. Don't make the interviewer hunt for information.

Pitching for interviews is a numbers game. If you make ten pitches, you may only receive one interview request. However, just because it's a numbers game doesn't mean you should treat hosts like numbers. They are busy people with a passion for what they do (and are often doing it as a labor of love, not a significant source of income). They love talking to interesting people. Show them that you are an interesting person who is worth interviewing.

If the host says no, thank them for their time and move on. Don't ask them to justify or reconsider their decision. Don't feel discouraged when you receive the inevitable rejections; that's part of the process.

And for those interviews you do land, we have some tips to make the most of the opportunity.

Preparing for Your Interview

An interviewer has accepted your pitch—congratulations! What additional preparation do you need to do to deliver a professional performance?

Provide any requested material immediately. Most interviewers will want a bio, a headshot, your website and social media links, and information about and links to any book associated with the topic of your conversation. We'll discuss this in more detail in the "Media Kit" section.

Make sure you have the host's email (and possibly phone number) in case of an emergency.

Manage your calendar. Accept any invitations the interviewer sends manually or via scheduling software. If you need to book the time manually on your end, include the interviewer as an invitee. If you're traveling to the interview—for example, to a local television or radio station—block out plenty of time before the interview itself. Even if it's a virtual event, block time before the interview so you can get settled and be calm and composed when the interview starts. For virtual events in which you are participating from home, also consider putting an entry on the calendars of anyone who might be at home with you when the interview takes place. This will encourage them to stay quiet during that time, and to refrain from high bandwidth computer activities if you are sharing a connection.

For virtual events, check to make sure that you have and are familiar with the meeting platform the host will be using (e.g., Zoom, StreamYard). If necessary to ensure a smooth interview experience, consider asking the host if you can set up a brief advance meeting with them to review the use of the platform.

Participating in the Interview

Arrive early for the interview. For an in-person interview, arrive half an hour before the scheduled interview start time (or earlier, if requested by the host). For virtual interviews, if you're familiar with the virtual meeting platform, sign in at least five minutes early to double-check your camera, microphone, and internet connection. If you're not familiar with the virtual meeting platform, sign in ten minutes early.

Expect to be a bit nervous. Some nervousness, rather than complacency, can prompt you to give a better interview. A skilled interviewer will have experience setting their guests at ease, and if you've prepared for the event (as any professional would), the knowledge that you're ready to deliver a valuable experience for your host and audience will moderate that nervousness.

During the interview, don't forget to smile—it will present a more appealing persona for your audience. This holds true even for audio-only interviews—listeners can hear a smile in your voice.

Don't forget to mention your book or the product or service you're promoting. Three mentions is a good rule of thumb—that's enough to fix the name in the listeners' or viewers' memories but not so much that it becomes annoying or self-serving. Your host won't appreciate it if you turn their event into an infomercial.

At the end of the interview, interviewers customarily ask something like, "Tell the audience where they can find out more about you." Make sure you have a clear 30-second pitch lined up. Direct people to your website, make sure you have links there to your social media sites, and mention what sites you're on, but *don't* exhaustively list every site and your profile name on each one.

Here's Matty's usual closing:

If listeners want more information about my suspense and thriller novels, they can go to MattyDalrymple.com—and that's Matty with a Y—and if they'd like more information about my non-fiction platform, they can go to TheIndyAuthor.com—and that's Indy with a Y. And I'd love to connect with them on Facebook at Matty Dalrymple or The Indy Author!

And here's a pro tip: don't waste syllables saying "www" in front of your URL. Just say your equivalent of *Matty Dalrymple dot com*.

Practice your closing until you can say it smoothly. This will be the last thing the audience hears, and possibly the one thing they will remember.

After the Interview

What you do after your interview is just as important as the pre-interview prep and your interview performance if you and your host are to gain maximum advantage from your talk.

One of Matty's pet peeves as an interviewer is when an interviewee goes to the trouble of crafting a pitch, scheduling the interview, providing the needed information (bio, headshot, social media links), preparing their material, and conducting the interview, and then goes radio silent. That's like driving to the beach, slogging through the sand, putting your surfboard in the water, and then walking away. Why bother?

First, send a thank you to your host for investing the time

and effort in helping you share your message with their audience.

Second, promote the event. It doesn't matter if your follower base is a fraction of your host's (or, for that matter, if your host's is a fraction of yours); it's just good form to promote your appearance and the host's platform enthusiastically. If you assume that the host will do all the work needed to share your knowledge with the right audience, you greatly reduce the likelihood that that host will ever invite you back for another interview, or ever recommend you as a guest to another host.

Do more than just liking or sharing the host's social media posts. Add a comment that will draw attention to the post (and ideally that provides even more value to the audience). Include links to the interview on your website. With the host's permission, repurpose the content to platforms the host might not reach.

Make sure your host knows you are promoting your appearance. Flag them in your social media posts or forward them a copy of your email newsletter. Promotion that is invisible to the host, or that they have to go hunting to find, does you no good in terms of paving the way to other interviews.

Finally, if your interview is recorded, commit to listening to or watching it so that you can capitalize on your strengths and address any weaknesses for subsequent interviews. For example, Matty's reviews of her performances as an interviewee remind her of the power of a sincere smile as well as the fact that a posture that might feel attentive to her can look grumpy or aggressive to a viewer.

Panels

Speaking engagements aren't limited to events where you are the solo speaker; panels also offer opportunities.

A panel is when a group of experts answers questions from a moderator and, in many cases, from the audience. Participants benefit from panels because different panelists can provide different perspectives on a topic. You generally do not need to prepare a presentation for a panel event, although the moderator may provide you with a list of likely questions in advance.

Participating in a panel is a great opportunity for community building, both with your fellow panelists and with the audience. Like an author newsletter swap, where you promote the books of other authors in exchange for their promotion of yours, panel discussions may introduce you and your work to a new audience. Panel discussions will be attended by people who have an interest in the topic being discussed, and who may know, or know of, one of your fellow panelists but not you. As a result, those attendees may become your fans and followers as well.

Panel participation is usually not an income generator. It's rarer to be paid for an appearance as a panelist than as a solo speaker, and if you *are* paid for a panel appearance, the fee will likely be low. This makes sense because you will need to do much less prep work for a panel than for a presentation. Income is more likely to come indirectly from attendees (and perhaps even fellow panelists) purchasing your books or otherwise availing themselves of your products and services. In addition, as with speakers, organizers sometimes waive event fees for panelists, so there can be a financial incentive to get placed on a panel at an event you want to attend anyway.

You must assess participation on a panel not only from a

professional but from a personal point of view. One of the primary requirements of being a successful panelist is the willingness to share the spotlight with others. If the idea of sharing a panel event with other authors—emphasis on *sharing*—makes you fidgety, then a panel is probably not right for you. However, if the idea of sharing the stage with others is comforting rather than cringe-worthy, then panel opportunities might be one of the first speaker engagements for you to pursue.

If the idea of participating in panels is appealing, consider the type of panel experience you want to pursue.

Finding Panel Opportunities

There are several ways of landing panel opportunities:

- If you register for an event that hosts panels, the registration form will often ask registrants if they are interested in speaking on a panel. If this isn't covered in the form, ask the organizers if panel opportunities are available.
- Membership in writers' groups or organizations can often lead to panel opportunities because event organizers often contact these groups for help identifying panelists for certain topics.
- Organizers will sometimes pull panelists from the speakers at the event. Michael and Matty participated on a panel on independent publishing held at a writers' conference where they were both giving solo talks.

Assessing Panel Opportunities

Finding a good match between the panel opportunities and your professional and personal preferences will greatly improve your panel performance and the benefits it can bring you and your audience. Ask the organizer to provide information on the topic, the moderator, the other panelists, and the logistics (e.g., a lightning round of questions or a leisurely conversation) to help you decide if a certain panel is one you want to join.

Topic

At events that are composed mainly or exclusively of panel events, organizers can't always make logical matches between the panelists and the topic. If an organizer has asked you to participate on a panel focused on a topic that is outside your normal repertoire, you will need to do a bit of research in advance or acknowledge that your contribution is going to be different from that of a fellow panelist who is an expert on the topic.

If the proposed panel topic is *far* outside your experience, it's probably best to alert the organizer to this, but even this doesn't mean you're disqualified from participating. For example, at one author conference, Matty was assigned to a panel focused on the portrayal of police in crime fiction and the moral dilemmas they face. She contacted the moderator and shared that her books were not police procedurals, but that one of her series did feature a police detective as a secondary character, and the fact that this character was engaging Matty's psychic protagonist to help solve a crime might itself be considered a moral dilemma. The moderator was happy to bake this angle into the discussion.

Structure

The more panelists on a panel, the less "airtime" each will have. Some organizers pack five, six, or even more authors on a panel, which means that each one gets only a few minutes to share their thoughts and to connect with the audience. Matty favors panels that include no more than four participants.

Moderator

Moderators play a critical role in the success of a panel. A moderator can ensure that participation is spread equitably across the panelists, and a skilled moderator can bring added value by reading the audience, directing the conversation, and bringing comments to a close when appropriate.

Consider whether the panel to which you have been invited will have a non-participant moderator. A moderator who is also acting as a panelist can't perform the moderator role as effectively, and this can impact the experience of both the audience and the panelists. At one event, Michael was on panels with five other people but no moderators. The panels were disasters for both the participants and the audience because there was no direction, and no one knew how to start or end the panel.

Other Panelists

If you don't know the fellow panelists or anything about them, this might be a moot point, but if you do, it's legitimate to consider if you want to share the stage with them (or if they'll want to share the stage with you). More on that in the next section.

The Hallmarks of a Panel Professional
The Professional Panelist

Being a panelist gives you a chance to connect with both audience members and your fellow panelists. This is going to be a successful connection only if you are a thoughtful and generous co-member of the panel. You will gain the respect of your fellow panelists and moderator, and a high likelihood of a repeat invitation to future panels, if you display the hallmarks of a panel professional.

- **Be positive**, **succinct**, and **respectful**.
- **Read the audience.** Adjust the content and language of your comments as appropriate for the

topic, venue, and audience. The moderator and audience of a panel focused on a hot-button political topic will expect, and accept, a much different kind of discussion than a panel focused on best indie publishing practices. Short-term attention gained by shock value or an intentionally offensive comment is likely to damage your long-term reputation.

- **Don't be a mic hog.** Matty remembers unfondly one panel where one of the participants hogged the microphone and that author's name has a black mark next to it in her mental Rolodex. Matty and this panelist had enough in common in their backgrounds as authors that a collaboration of some sort might otherwise have been a possibility, but Matty won't work with an author whose only goal is to promote themselves at the expense of others. Matty spoke to some of the attendees after the event, and their comments about that author were not positive. Far from winning over followers, this panelist shut down possible connections with their behavior.
- **Don't be mic shy.** Even if you are early in your author career and are on a panel with more experienced panelists, the audience still expects to hear from you and to gain value from your contribution. Be sure you go into the panel event prepared to hold up your end of the bargain.
- The panel experience should be a **free-flowing conversation** among the moderator and the panelists, and you can help create that environment. Be the author who directs questions to a fellow panelist when appropriate. Don't be

afraid to offer an alternative perspective on information another panelist has shared—the audience will benefit from hearing multiple sides of an issue—but make sure to frame your position respectfully.

The Professional Moderator

All the advice about not hogging the spotlight as a panelist applies double as a moderator. If you're moderating a panel, your job is to elicit the best results from the panelists and to serve the audience, not to promote yourself, build your own community, or create income.

Serving as a moderator can entail a lot of work; for example, you may need to research the panelists or read some of their work. Factor in this time investment when weighing the benefits of accepting a moderator role. That said, acting as a moderator can be a great opportunity to network with the panelists and to build goodwill with the organizers. Weigh the pros and cons carefully.

If you have an opportunity to moderate a panel and decide to accept, here are some tips:

- Don't march through a list of pre-prepared questions (unless that's the expectation the organizer has set). You might start out with a prepared question, but then see where the conversation goes. Guide it within the boundaries of the panel's advertised topic.
- Consider whether or not to give the panelists the questions in advance. There are advantages to either option.
- The advantage of providing the questions in advance is that it gives the panelists a chance to

think through their thoughts or positions on a question. They can provide more carefully constructed responses and can avoid rambling answers. If the panelist is not entirely comfortable in front of an audience, having the questions in advance can set them at ease. And if you've unintentionally wandered into a sensitive area with your questions, they can alert you in advance, saving you and the panelist embarrassment.
- The advantage of *not* providing the questions in advance is that it can encourage more organic conversation, and spontaneous answers are often more interesting and engaging than rehearsed responses.

If you're unsure what the appropriate approach is for a particular panel, consider asking the panelists what they prefer. If all of them are comfortable with not having the questions in advance, the decision is easy. If some of them want the questions in advance, then provide the questions in advance to *all* the panelists.

- Make sure all the panelists have equal airtime, which means being prepared to manage any mic hogs. Use subtle prompts, like asking another panelist for their opinion on what the mic hog said, or even unsubtle prompts like, "Let's hear from the other panelists …"
- If you're moderating a large panel, you may need to pose each question to only a sub-set of the panelists. If you need to use this approach, be sure to let the panelists know this in advance so they

won't think you've forgotten about them when you don't ask them to answer a question. You also need to make sure that each panelist gets the opportunity to address approximately the same number of questions. You can monitor this by having a list of panelists and discreetly putting a mark next to the name when you ask that panelist a question.

- If you throw a question out to the whole panel, don't automatically call on the first panelist who puts their hand up in response. Some people will have an answer immediately and some will need a few moments to think about it. Give the panelists several seconds to consider the question before choosing your first respondent.
- Vary the order in which you pose the questions to the panelists. If you always start at one end of the table and work your way down, the person at the end of the table is too often going to have to answer, "What they said." Rotate who gets the first shot at answering the question.
- If an event organizer is not in the room for the panel discussion, you as the moderator might need to take on other responsibilities, such as ensuring enough chairs are available for attendees or addressing climate control issues.

Moderating virtual events:

- For virtual events, you may also have to keep an eye on the live chat for questions. This will require you to listen to the panelists as well as read the chat, which requires supreme

multitasking abilities. If that feels overwhelming, ask the organizer to provide someone to help you with that.
- A good way to avoid having multiple virtual panelists start talking at the same time is to ask all panelists to mute themselves, and to unmute when they have something to say. This is a subtle way of "raising a virtual hand," and you can call on one of the panelists who have unmuted.

Dealing with Unprofessional Participants

The tips above will help you manage problematic panelists as a moderator. But even as a panelist, you should be prepared to deal with other panelists who may not have made the same commitment to professionalism that you have.

If you find yourself on a panel with an unprofessional panelist, stay keenly aware of your facial expressions—don't get drawn into the bad vibe they are creating by letting your frustration show. If the audience shares your frustration, then the unprofessional participant will earn their karmic ire. If they don't share your frustration, then reflecting your frustration will make you seem small-minded.

If the panel has a moderator, it's generally best to let that person handle the situation, but if the moderator isn't dealing with the situation effectively, you as a panelist might be able to help them out. Although using humor to lighten the mood can be tempting, it brings with it the risk that the transgressor will take offense and escalate the situation. Redirecting the conversation to another topic is often the safest course.

Workshops

Workshops are another type of talk you can consider for your professional speaker portfolio.

In a workshop, you work in-depth with participants on a certain topic, sometimes over an extended period. A workshop can be completely interactive with no presentation, or it can have a presentation element that you refer to throughout the talk. If you incorporate a presentation in the workshop, reference the information in the section on "Preparing Your Talk."

In this section, we focus on workshops managed by event organizers—for example, Michael and Matty presented a workshop on independent publishing at a conference at the invitation of Writer's Digest. We do not address the process of developing and deploying a workshop from scratch, which could itself be the subject of an entire book.

Consider the Experience

Workshops can be one of the most intensive and interactive types of events a professional speaker can undertake. When assessing workshop opportunities, consider the length of the workshop and your ability to maintain the needed level of energy for the duration. In Matty's corporate life, she facilitated workshops that lasted two days; these always involved a second facilitator, which gave her opportunities for some downtime to recharge. Similarly, the Writer's Digest workshop Matty and Michael facilitated was a day long, but they alternated topics.

Consider the Medium

The fact that workshops are often led by more than one person sets them apart from most other types of speaker engagements. Even panels, although they involve multiple speakers, usually don't require extensive coordination among the speakers (except, perhaps, in the case of the moderator).

If you're facilitating a workshop with another person, then it's vital that you have a clear agreement on roles and responsibilities. Who will act as primary contact with the organizer? Who is responsible for creating any needed presentation materials? What consistent format will you use? Co-facilitating a workshop is like co-writing a book; be prepared to set the stage for a cooperative partnership.

Consider the Benefits

Workshops are one of the most expensive types of speaking engagements to execute. They are complex to develop, and so carry a high time expense, and often require travel, which carries a financial expense. On the other hand, because organizers recognize this dynamic, speakers can often command higher fees for workshops than for standard presentations. Furthermore, because of the intensive nature of workshops, they are a great way to forge strong bonds with participants, and to win life-long fans and followers.

Author Readings

You may not associate author readings with a speaking career, but they do involve performing in front of an in-person or virtual audience and can involve panel-like Q&A sessions. They can serve the goals of earning income, especially if the event includes the opportunity to sell books, and of building community with fellow authors and with readers.

When you pursue or accept an invitation to share your work in an author reading, you owe the organizer and the audience the same professionalism you would for any other speaking engagement. In this section, we share some tips for what that means for an author reading, and how you can optimize the experience for yourself as well.

We focus on events where you are reading with other

authors. With solo readings, such as you might include in a book launch event, you have more flexibility, but since you are acting as your own organizer, much of this information applies in that scenario as well.

Selecting Your Material

The organizer of a reading event determines the type of experience they want themselves, the readers, and the audience to have; be sure to comply with their direction. Adherence to their guidelines will provide the best experience for everyone involved and will increase your chances of getting invited back for future readings.

If the organizer specifies a theme, be sure your material fits. Don't show up for a reading advertised as light comedy with a selection from your noir work-in-progress.

Organizers can provide guidance regarding the venue and audience, which should inform the material you select for your reading. But keep in mind that the organizer might not have complete control over who will hear your reading. For example, these events are often held in restaurant event rooms connected to the dining room, where there might be young children. Matty once attended a reading held in the early evening in a private room at a family-friendly shopping center restaurant where one author read a fairly graphic S&M scene. That scene might have been fine for another venue—perhaps a city bar late at night—but it was not right for that event.

Similarly, consider the language. Some of the scenes Matty uses for readings contain profanity, and she will read those as written for an adult audience in a bar but substitute a less vulgar word if she's reading at a library on a Sunday morning (especially if it's in a location where children might be listening in). Select your material appropriately for the venue and audience.

Organizers will provide a time limit for your reading; a

common time limit is five to seven minutes for each author. If you are reading from a prose work, this is likely not enough time to share an entire story; it may not even be enough time to read an entire chapter of a novel. You will need to select an excerpt that will meet the needs of the organizer and the audience. If the event is focused on crime fiction, your reading should include some criminal aspect. If the event is focused on thrillers, consider leaving your audience with a cliffhanger. (You can ensure the audience has a way of finding out the resolution to the cliff-hanger—and gain some book sales—by pointing them to the work from which the reading was taken, perhaps even offering a special discount for attendees.) On the other hand, if you are reading poetry or even micro fiction, you may be able to share an entire work in your allotted time.

We can't emphasize this enough: respect the time constraints the organizer provides. We've seen authors blow past the time limit for a reading who are then offended when the organizer cuts them off. Overshooting your allotted time is disrespectful to everyone. Organizers impose time limits for a reason. They may be constrained by limits set by the venue—for example, a restaurant might need to close by a certain time. Audience members have an expectation of event duration. Each author deserves their allotted time, and any reader who overruns their time eats into the time of authors later in the agenda.

Ensuring that the material you have selected for your reading meets the organizer's specified time limit is part of the preparation process. How do you ensure that you can read your selected passage within the time allocated to your reading? Guesstimates based on word count or number of pages are not sufficient. The only way to know how long a selection will take is to read it aloud and time it.

Prepping Your Performance

Don't assume that because you wrote the words you can automatically perform the reading. As any speaker engagement, practice is the key to providing the best performance.

Never try to hit a time limit by talking faster. You want your audience to be able to savor your carefully crafted words, and they won't be able to do that if they're hearing them at double speed. If you time your selection and it's running long, shorten your script. A well-presented four-minute piece is going to be far more enjoyable for the audience—and for you—than a rushed eight-minute piece.

From what format should you read? Reading from your phone, tablet, or laptop might be tempting, but you open yourself to all the usual risks of electronic devices: a rapidly depleting battery, a venue with no cell service and no Wi-Fi, or a finger flick that scrolls further than you want, leaving you fumbling to find your spot. Reading from a print book looks cool but is logistically challenging. The print is usually too small, pages can be hard to turn, and notes are difficult to incorporate.

Matty recommends printing out your material on card stock, available at any office supply store. This paper is thicker than normal printer paper but can be fed through a standard home office printer. It's easier to handle—for example, easier to turn one page at a time—and more durable. Be sure to number the pages in case they get out of order and you need to reassemble them.

Be prepared to *perform*, not just read, your material. Some degree of dramatization—even for readings of non-fiction works—will win over your audience. Consider color-coding dialogue based on the character who is speaking, especially if you have long passages of dialogue. This will ensure you use the right voice for each character.

Listening to a recording of yourself reading the material is the only way of getting a true sense of your performance. For one reading, Matty thought she was delivering quite a dramatic rendition, but when she listened to the recording, it sounded monotone. Conversely, the recording might also clue you in if you're going overboard on the drama (although this is a far less common problem).

For scenes including dialogue, you can also confirm if your differentiation of the characters' voices is sufficient to be able to identify the characters. This might enable you to leave out some of the dialogue tags ("he said / she said"), since your reading doesn't have to match the print version exactly. Also be sure to leave pauses between different speakers' lines of dialogue.

Listening to a recording of yourself performing the reading will also likely convince you that you can read much more slowly and pause much more frequently than might be your natural inclination. It's rare to hear a reader read too slowly, but if you are one of the few for which this is the issue, listening to your recording, and perhaps soliciting input from others, will let you know to what extent you need to pick up the tempo.

Listen to the recording a few times to familiarize yourself with the material. This will enable you to maximize eye contact with the audience. If your eyes are glued to the page, it's not only less engaging for the audience, but also harder for them to hear you.

Being super familiar with the material paid off for Matty at one reading where, part-way through the first page, she realized that due to the set-up of the lectern and the microphone, she could only see the top two-thirds of the page unless she awkwardly shifted the page up and down to see the remaining third. She basically read the last third of every page from memory. Being thoroughly familiar with the material meant her audience was not even aware of the issue.

Delivering the Reading

Never begin a reading with a preemptive apology. There is nothing more depressing for an audience than to hear authors preface their readings with, "I've never done this before, so bear with me," or "I'm not going to be as good as that last reader." We suspect people do this because they figure if they set the bar low enough, even a mediocre performance will exceed expectations. However, it's more likely that, in anticipation of a lackluster performance, the audience members will get out their phones to check social media, or head to the bar for another beer.

Even worse than the reader who issues a preemptive apology for their performance is the reader who admits to lack of preparation: "I didn't get a chance to practice this much before today ..." That does nothing but reflect disrespect for your audience. If your reading is five minutes long and if you have an audience of twenty, you are using one hundred minutes of your audience's (and potential readers') time. Spend the time needed to ensure that your audience will have a satisfying hundred minutes; careful preparation will give you the confidence not to fall back on these types of excuses.

Close strong and simple. Never conclude a reading with "that's it" or "that's all" or other self-deprecating comment. Look up from your notes, smile, say "thank you," and provide a brief reminder of the source of the reading and, if appropriate, where audience members can find it. ("That was from the Ann Kinnear Suspense Novel *The Sense of Death*, and I'll be selling signed copies during the breaks.") Then depart the stage knowing that you delivered a great experience for your organizer and your audience!

Being a Good Audience Member

At a multi-author reading, you have a responsibility as an audience member as well as a reader. Stay for the entire event. Arrive in time to hear the first reader and stay until the last reader is done. There's nothing more discouraging to readers scheduled late in an event to see other readers exit once their own readings are done. Show those readers the same courtesy they showed you by being an attentive audience for their performance. (And use this time to your benefit by noting the most compelling readers' best practices you can emulate, as well as the least compelling readers' worst practices you should avoid.)

Reaping the Benefits

As with most author speaking engagements, readings are a great way to network with the event organizer, perhaps leading to additional gigs, and with fellow authors. And, of course, readings offer a great opportunity to connect with enthusiastic readers, especially if the event is genre specific. If the organizer and venue permit it, be sure to have your books on offer. You might have print copies available, or point audience members to an electronic format, perhaps via a QR code on a business card or small flyer.

Keynotes

A keynote is a presentation involving one speaker whose goal is to motivate and inspire. Keynotes can share many characteristics with non-keynote presentations, such as the use of slides. (Slides are not required for a keynote but can make the talk more engaging. Michael once saw Jack Hanna deliver an amazing keynote speech that included slides illustrating his work as an animal rights activist and zookeeper.)

The main differentiators between a keynote and a more standard presentation are:

- The level of formality around the event - Graduation speeches and after-dinner speeches at galas are classic examples of keynotes.
- The more scripted nature of the delivery - Keynotes are the only type of talk where even the most experienced speakers often use notes, and these notes are often more of a script than would be appropriate in other talks. This use of a script means you generally have less flexibility to make adjustments on the fly.
- The script - When creating your script, don't be limited by correct grammar--insert commas where you want to remember to pause for a beat. Also consider inserting timestamps (10 mins, 15 mins) based on your practice sessions so that you can adjust your pacing as needed throughout. Consider marking sections that you can skip over if your speech is running long or sections that you can optionally include if your speech is running short.
- The pace - Keynotes are generally delivered at a slower pace than other types of talks.
- No Q&A - Keynotes generally do not include a Q&A, but be prepared to engage with event attendees afterward to address any questions or extend the conversation.

Keynotes are generally the purview of speakers with long résumés of successful performances, and they are generally not an option for those earlier in their speaker careers. More so than with other types of talks, speakers are more likely to be invited to provide a keynote than to have to apply for the opportunity. A robust professional network and exemplary professionalism will pave the way to such invitations.

Once you qualify for invitations to provide keynotes, you can expect the earning potential to expand far beyond what's usual for more standard presentations.

Speaker's Notes

Capture your responses to the questions below in the downloadable document available at https://www.theindyauthor.com/from-page-to-platform.html.

- Which type of "not the usual suspects" talks—interviews / podcasts, panels, workshops, author readers, and keynotes—most appeals to you?
- Why do you find that type of talk most appealing? This might inform your speaker goals.
- For that type of talk, who are three organizers to whom you might pitch yourself as a speaker?

FORMATS: IN-PERSON AND VIRTUAL

In addition to the types of talks you want to consider for your author career, you also want to consider the pros and cons of different formats—in-person and virtual—and how they match up with your professional goals and personal preferences.

At one time, events were by definition in person, and our options for the events we participated in were constrained by the distance we were willing and able to travel. Event organizers had to draw their roster of speakers from experts available in the local area, had to budget money to bring speakers to the venue, or had to ask the speakers to fund the travel themselves.

In-person events can support all the speaker goals we describe in the section on "Types of Talks ... Not Just the Usual Suspects" but are especially valuable if your goals include building community. Of course if travel is a goal, then in-person events are the ones you'll want to pursue. In-person events are generally more energizing than virtual events. These are the events whose memories stick with us long after the event is over.

But don't underestimate the value of virtual events. Geography is no longer a limiter, and event organizers can draw their roster of speakers—including professional speakers like you—from anywhere in the world. Except for travel, virtual events can support all goals we describe in the section "Defining Your Goals as a Speaker." The goal of building community is definitely within reach—you may just need to work a little harder at this with a virtual event than with an in-person event. And if your goals include earning income, virtual events might be preferable because they remove the need to negotiate or cover travel costs.

With both options available, you need to understand the advantages of each, and how each can support your goals for your speaking career.

There are four primary considerations for which type of event you prioritize based on your goals:

- the **time required from you** to execute an engagement
- the **money required from you** to execute an engagement
- the **speaker experience** you seek for yourself
- the **audience connection** you want to forge

We explore these below.

In-person Events

Time

Traveling to in-person events will take more time than just strolling into your home office for a virtual event. Furthermore, the event as a whole will take more time because you're generally not committed just for the duration of your talk, but for the duration of the event. Therefore, in-person events can be more difficult to fit into your schedule, especially if you're juggling your speaker career with a full-time job or with family commitments.

The time investment needed to travel to in-person events can be more onerous for some speakers than for others. For example, Matty lives outside Philadelphia, with easy access to air and rail services that offer extensive scheduling options. If she misses a connection, an alternative is just hours, or even minutes, away. Michael, however, lives in Iowa, far from rail services and with access to only limited flight options. If Michael misses a connection, he can be delayed for a full day, possibly more. This means that when he's assessing the return on his time investment to speak at an in-person event, he must consider not only the best-case travel scenario but also the probability that he will be spending an unplanned night away from home. (That means not only lost time but also lost income since it's an expense that an event organizer is unlikely to cover.)

Each speaker's calculus related to weighing the time cost of in-person events will be different. Because Michael is managing his author and speaker work alongside a full-time corporate job, he calculates the time cost of in-person events not only in terms of their impact on his writing productivity but also in terms of the time he must take off from work.

Matty, as a full-time author, publisher, and podcaster, is less concerned about the time impact of attending an in-person event because the benefits she is likely to gain in all three of those areas almost always justify the time allocated to the event.

The key is to consider whether the extra time required for an in-person event will compensate you by supporting your speaker goals.

Money

The amount of money you can *earn* from in-person events does not necessarily differ from the amount you can earn from virtual events. The money consideration is related more to the *costs* incurred for accepting an in-person engagement.

The costs of traveling to an in-person event can be significant: a bus, airline, or train ticket, gas and wear-and-tear on your own vehicle, meals, and even incidentals. (Why does toothpaste always cost more when you're on the road than when you're shopping at your local drug store?)

You may be able to negotiate coverage of travel expenses into your speaker contract, but organizers can't possibly cover every cost (see the section on "Travel Costs" for more on that). Even if they could, your travel would still not be free: your time is money, too.

If the event organizers are *not* footing your travel bill, then money factors even more strongly into your decision to pursue or accept in-person engagements.

Matty favors engagements she can drive to in Chiclet, her Ford Transit Connect mobile writing retreat. Not only does she save on expenses like airfare, but she can bring most of what she needs with her, saving expenses such as shipping books to a venue. In a pinch, she can even sleep in Chiclet— she's done it before. (More on that later.)

Michael calculates the financial impact of an in-person gig based not only on the fee he will receive for his talk and the direct costs of getting to the venue, but other financial factors such as being able to write off travel expenses on his taxes. In fact, there are other financial benefits of funding your own travel. You might receive credit card bonus points, frequent flyer miles, ticket upgrades, free rooms, and other perks. These not only represent tangible financial benefits, perhaps defraying the costs of a future trip to an in-person event, but they also make your travel experience much more comfortable.

Speaker Experience

Another consideration when weighing in-person versus virtual events is the experience you want for yourself as the speaker.

At in-person events, you are usually on a stage, and when you speak, all eyes are on you. If you love the attention and energy that being in the same space as your audience provides, then in-person events can't be beat. In fact, the ability to command a room is such a vital part of being a professional author speaker that we encourage you to pursue some in-person events even if the thought of being on a stage intimidates you. Every room has energy, and as a speaker, you will feed off it. You may find you love it!

In-person events also make it easier for you to gauge how the audience is receiving your talk and adjust accordingly. The audience may even take your talk in directions you didn't anticipate, and although you should be prepared to redirect it back to your planned topic if needed, you should also be open to the opportunity to explore that new direction if you feel it would be beneficial for your audience. It may highlight a possible area for improvement for future iterations of that talk, or even add a new topic to your repertoire of talks.

And even the largest in-person venues can provide an opportunity to connect with people one-on-one, whether it be answering a question from the stage or chatting with someone after your talk. Such connections can be valuable personally as well as professionally, especially for those of us who spend most of our time in the usually solitary work of authors.

If you thrive on these types of interpersonal interactions, then the benefits of in-person events are clear. But even as introverts who spend most of our days working from home,

Michael and Matty both recognize the benefits of getting out of the house and interacting with others—especially those who share our interests.

Audience Connection

Another question to ask yourself when deciding on the pros and cons of in-person events is about the type of connection you want to forge with your audience.

If you are speaking on a topic with emotional depth—for example, the experience of recovering from addiction or advice on improving family relationships—then the emotional connection you establish with your audience will be a key component of the success of your talk.

It's far easier to forge these connections if you can look your audience in the eye, and far easier to make on-the-fly adjustments to your presentation or style if you can read an actual room. You also gain energy from an energized audience, which can make your message even more effective.

And your opportunity to build connections with your audience doesn't end when you step off the podium. You can poll audience members for their reaction to your presentation or for clarifications they might need that you can feed into its next iteration, an opportunity that is much more difficult to capitalize on in a virtual event.

If you have the time and money to invest in attendance at an in-person event, if you hope to use the event as an opportunity to build your network, and if your message, topic, or style benefits from the depth of the connection you can form with your audience, consider favoring in-person events for your speaking engagements.

Virtual Events

Time

A virtual event gives you access to a global audience from the comfort of your home or office, with little time investment needed beyond that required to prepare for and give the talk itself.

Time is the primary reason that, even before the pandemic, Matty temporarily reduced her in-person appearances. Her fiction work was the primary income-earner in her author portfolio, and any activity that took time away from her work on her novel in progress felt hard to justify from a cost-benefit perspective. Participation in virtual events left practically an entire day to devote to fiction writing.

And Michael is never going to miss a connection or spend an extra night away from his family if his "travel" to a virtual event involves getting from his kitchen to his office.

In terms of efficiency, virtual events win, hands down.

Money

As noted above, speaker's *fees* do not necessarily differ between in-person and virtual events. Sometimes you may earn more money speaking virtually. The money consideration is related more to the *costs* you incur for each type of event. With virtual events, you obviously save the travel expenses required by in-person events, but there are a few expenses that you'll need to consider.

One is your internet service. To participate at a professional level in virtual events, you must have a robust connection to provide high quality audio and video. You will have put a lot of work into your talk—you'll want to make sure that the sound and images you broadcast to the attendees are just as good. The best way to ensure a high-quality connection is to use a wired Ethernet port; if you don't have one, it's worth the money to hire an electrician to install one in your home.

Another expense is audiovisual equipment. As we will cover in more depth in the section on "Creating a Virtual Presentation Space," you should use an auxiliary camera and microphone—not those built into your computer—for a professional presentation.

Speaker Experience

The mechanics of virtual talks are simple. You sign on to the meeting platform in advance of the presentation as directed by the host, you deliver your presentation, and then you sign off. You may never even see or hear from your audience. Some events may even be prerecorded with no audience.

If you're uncomfortable with the idea of speaking in front of an audience, this might seem like a benefit, but you lose the energy and instant feedback that an audience provides. This lack of human interaction is one of the biggest drawbacks of virtual events.

Enlist the organizer or event facilitator to help address this downside. In a live event, establish an agreement with them ahead of time about how they will feed audience comments to you or alert you if participants seem confused. If your presentation will be prerecorded, ask the organizer / facilitator to act as your audience. Even if they never appear onscreen, knowing that there's an actual person receiving your message in the moment will give you more energy than if you're talking to a blank screen or glowing recording light.

Because of the ease of attendance, participants in virtual events may also represent a wider spectrum of cultures and possibly different interpretations and expectations. Michael was once presenting a talk he had given dozens of times to an audience that was mostly non-American. Michael mentioned one of his books at the beginning of the talk and gave what he thought was a very light sales pitch, but the audience didn't see it that way. For the rest of the talk, the chat was filled with complaints about him being a pushy American. This is a reminder to keep cultural norms in mind when preparing your presentation.

If you can, ask the organizer to review your slides for any items that might not land properly with their audience due to cultural differences. Otherwise, these cultural lessons will often be learned through trial and error. While uncomfortable, getting tested by global audiences is actually a great way to sharpen your speaking skills.

Audience Connection

A vital consideration for a preference of virtual versus in-person events is the type of connection you want to form with your audience.

Virtual events are perfect for reaching as wide an audience as possible. Whereas in-person events might range from a dozen (or less) to several hundred, virtual events can draw a global audience of thousands. When you consider that replays of these events are often made available on video platforms such as YouTube, you could potentially reach millions over time.

Virtual events also lend themselves to talks that are more fact-based rather than emotion- or experience-based. For example, when Matty gives talks on the mechanics of indie publishing short fiction, she doesn't need to form an emotional bond with attendees in order to convey the benefits of using templated covers or to describe how the processes that an indie author uses to publish a novel-length work can be applied to short fiction. In fact, the ease of sharing supporting visuals on a virtual platform is another benefit of this approach for this type of fact-based topic.

Speaker's Notes

Capture your responses to the questions below in the downloadable document available at https://www.theindyauthor.com/from-page-to-platform.html.

- Is your **time** limited by other commitments (which might favor virtual events), or do you have the bandwidth to invest in attending the event (which might favor in-person events)?
- Is the **money** you need to invest to participate in an event a limiter? (If yes, favor virtual over in-person events.)
- Is the **speaker experience** a driver of your desire to develop a speaker career? Do you feed off the energy of an audience? Is community building high on your list of goals? (If yes, in-person events will be a better fit for you.)
- What type of **audience connection** do you need to establish? (Consider whether your goal is to share information, which can be done easily and with a large audience via a virtual event, or whether it is to establish an emotional connection, which is better done in person.)
- Based on your answers to these questions, which event format seems like a better match to your goals: in-person or virtual?

FINDING THE OPPORTUNITIES

Now that you understand the goals of your speaking career, the goals of your talk, the types of talks available to you, and the pros and cons of in-person versus virtual events, where will you look for opportunities to pitch yourself for the types of engagements that are the best match?

Keep a list of the most promising leads and set a reminder on your calendar to follow up with each one based on when organizers will be planning speakers for their next event. For example, Matty has a list of annual writers' conferences for which she wants to pitch herself as a speaker, and about a month after the conclusion of one year's conference, she contacts the organizers about the following year's conference, then adjusts further follow-up based on when organizers tell her they will be considering speakers.

Your Author and Speaker Communities

One of the best ways to find speaker opportunities is to be an active member of your author community and of your growing speaker community. Let them know that you're seeking speaking engagements. Build a media kit and post it on a page with an easy-to-remember URL you can share with colleagues. (We'll provide more details about this in the "Media Kit" section.) If you're interested in doing author readings, writers' groups are an especially valuable source for those engagements.

Expand your community based on your topic. Have a book on birdwatching? Seek out groups and organizations focused on that topic and alert them to your speaking services. Don't restrict yourself only to local groups—thanks to virtual platforms, it's as easy (and sometimes easier) to speak to a birdwatching group across the country as in your hometown.

Conferences

Conferences are a key source of speaking opportunities, and they provide an easy way of matching opportunities with your focus. Stay in touch with colleagues who have spoken at a conference at which you want to be a speaker. They can provide helpful information about the application and selection process. (You might expect these people to withhold information, since you may be vying for the same limited number of speaker slots, but no group is as generous in helping their fellow professionals as authors.)

Conferences will sometimes assemble panels from event attendees, so if you're interested in participating on panels, be sure to keep an eye out for this option when you register for the conference.

Placement Services

We have put placement services last in our list of options for finding opportunities for speaking engagements because we have found these to be the least effective approach, especially for those early in their speaking careers. However, it's valuable to be aware of these services so that you can capitalize on the low- or no-cost options and assess the for-cost options armed with our cautionary notes.

Online "matchmaking services" provide a means of matching speakers with organizers and vice versa—in the podcasting world, these include services like Matchmaker.fm and PodcastGuests.com. Speakers can search the service's directory for podcasts looking for guests, and organizers / hosts can search the directory for guests or speakers who are experts in a desired topic. The list of matchmaking services is ever-changing so doing a periodic online search for current contenders is your best bet. Try searching for *how to find speakers* or *how to find interview guests* and filter results to the past year to discover where organizers and hosts are looking for speakers.

A few of these services offer a free plan with access to a limited directory, a limited number of pitches or contacts, and a stripped-down speaker bio section. If you have the time to invest in exploring them, they can be a good "why not?" option. However, fewer and fewer services are offering a free plan.

Paid plans can be pricey, sometimes running to thousands of dollars. Because these plans often charge a flat fee for a certain number of placements, they are incentivized to pitch you to organizers and hosts even if the match isn't a perfect fit. Another downside of these services is that by working through an intermediary, you're reducing the personal connection you want to establish with event organizers / hosts. Matty deprioritizes pitches for guests for The Indy Author Podcast that come via matchmaking services because it's more difficult for her to judge whether the potential guest is a good match personality-wise.

Speakers' bureaus are another flavor of placement service, matching professional speakers with organizers, events, and venues. Unlike the types of matchmaking services described above, speakers' bureaus usually charge not a flat fee but rather a percentage of the speaking fee. They will often negotiate the contract for the engagement, and in some cases may also provide marketing and promotional support to their roster of client speakers, as well as logistical support, such as arranging travel.

Speaker's bureaus usually engage speakers who already have an established speaking career, or who qualify as a celebrity for some other reason. (They are often a source for keynote speakers.) For this reason, they are often not a realistic option for speakers at the beginning of their careers. In fact, even someone we would consider an A-list speaker decided not to pursue use of a speakers' bureau because they didn't feel they could command a high enough fee for the service: "Unless you can easily get $5k+ for a keynote, I'm not sure a bureau would take you on."

Another possible downside of using a speakers' bureau is that some require that all "their" speakers' engagements be booked through them and at their rates, which might prevent you from offering discounted or pro bono talks that you want to accept for professional or personal reasons.

However, writers' groups, especially ones with a national or international presence, sometimes offer speakers' bureau services to their author members, and these services may well be free of charge (more a vetted list of speakers than a full speakers' bureau service). Research the groups that make sense based on your topic area to identify opportunities.

A final type of placement service are PR firms. These

have the same downsides as the matchmaker services describe above, as well as the downside that they do not necessarily specialize in speaker opportunities (e.g., a PR firm that focuses on helping authors find more readers will not necessarily have the contacts or expertise to help speakers find speaking engagements).

Of course, some speakers have had great luck with all of these types of placement services, but especially early in your speaker career we recommend that you prioritize the other options for finding opportunities that we describe in this section.

Speaker's Notes

Capture your responses to the questions below in the downloadable document available at https://www.theindyauthor.com/from-page-to-platform.html.

- What are the top three approaches to finding opportunities that you will prioritize for landing speaking engagements?
- Who is a writer colleague who has spoken at, or at least attended, a conference to which you would like to pitch yourself for an engagement? (Make a plan to meet with them over coffee—actual or virtual—in the next week.)

ASSESSING THE OPPORTUNITIES

In this section, we outline the general considerations for assessing opportunities: the organizer's goals, the organizer's / event's professionalism, and the venue. If you are seeking opportunities, you will need to factor in these considerations when deciding to whom to pitch your speaker services. If you are lucky enough to be approached with opportunities, you will need to factor these in when deciding whether to accept the offer.

When you're first starting out on your speaking career, you might be tempted to pitch yourself for every event and to accept every offer that comes your way. But every speaking engagement you take on means something you give up, whether that's the ability to accept a different (and perhaps more desirable) engagement, time on your work in progress, or a well-earned break from your author business. It's hard to say no, but sometimes it's the right answer, and it's helpful to establish your criteria for acceptance ahead of time so you have a measure by which to assess your opportunities.

In the section on "Defining Your Goals as a Speaker," we discussed the importance of **understanding your own**

goals for your speaker career: direct and indirect income, learning, paying it forward, community-building, and so on. Assess each opportunity against its ability to move you toward your primary goals. For example, if you have a goal of creating direct income, podcast interviews probably won't meet the criteria since most podcast guests are not paid for their appearances. However, if your goal is indirect income, then landing a podcast interview on the topic of a book you want to promote is a perfect match. Eliminate opportunities that won't support your goals and prioritize the ones that will.

We also discussed the importance of assessing opportunities for how well they will support **your goals for your audience**. If you want to educate your audience about how to navigate the publishing voyage as an independent author, then a virtual meeting with the members of a writers' group will be a good target. If you want your audience to support a charitable organization that holds deep meaning for you, then an in-person event might work better to establish that rapport.

The final stakeholder whose goals you must consider is the organizer, and we consider that next.

Consider the Organizer's Goals

What is the **organizer** of an event hoping to achieve? Are they hoping to educate an audience? To serve a special interest? To win people to their position?

Make sure that what you have to offer aligns with what the organizers are looking for. The best way to do this for events that are held regularly, like an annual conference, is to be an attendee before you pitch yourself as a speaker. If this isn't possible, research the event and speak with the organizer to determine their goals and what they're looking for in a speaker. No matter how good a fit an opportunity is with your goals for yourself, it's not good form—or a good use of your time—to pitch yourself and your talk if they don't meet the organizer's goals.

For example, as the host of The Indy Author Podcast, Matty's goal is to serve her audience by sharing information that will support them with their writing craft and their publishing voyage—not to sell them products or services. She has hosted many guests who offer such products or services, but the ground rule is that the conversation must be of value to the listeners even if they don't purchase the product or service. (She always gives the guest an opportunity for a brief pitch at the end of the interview.) A guest who approaches the interview with a selling rather than an educating mindset is not likely to get a repeat invitation.

Having already identified the opportunities that will support your goals for yourself and for your audience, you can approach the right organizers with compelling pitches that factor in their goals as well.

Consider the Organizer's and Event's Professionalism

Is the organizer / event one with which you want to align yourself? Have the organizers published information about their expectations for the event and for its attendees? Do they have a formal statement regarding how they will handle issues such as harassment? (Formal guidelines on such subjects are more common for large, highly managed events than for small, informal events.) Does an online search suggest these guidelines have ever been invoked? How did the organizers handle such situations? Has the event or organizer been embroiled in any controversies? How did they handle these?

A simple web search will help you uncover issues you should know about, and don't forget to tap into the experiences of friends or colleagues who have attended the event previously.

Consider the Venue

By "venue," we mean the actual or virtual setting of the event.

If the venue is **actual**, location is an obvious consideration. You will need to budget more time and money to participate in an event held in another state or another country than in one held in your hometown. The venue itself is a consideration—for example, reviews might comment on the condition of the facility or the demeanor of the staff.

For example, Matty once spoke at an event in New England held during an unseasonably warm November. When she got to her hotel room, it was oppressively warm. A visit to the reception desk revealed that the hotel turned off its air conditioning on November 1 and that the only way to cool the room would be to have maintenance open the window and then return to close it as needed. Matty was able to get a room at another hotel for one night of the conference and spent the other two nights in Chiclet the Mobile Writing Retreat. (You know a room is uncomfortable when a cot in the back of a Ford Transit is a more appealing option.) She no longer pitches herself as a speaker at events held at that venue.

If the venue is **virtual**, consider what meeting platform is being used. Is it one you're comfortable with? You don't want your first experience with a platform to be as a presenter.

For example, Matty was invited to speak at a virtual conference for which speakers would use a multi-platform streaming service for their talks. Matty had never used the platform before and in fact had never been an attendee at an event that was organized the way this event was organized. As she considered the learning curve needed to execute the presentation—understanding and managing the multi-platform streaming service as well as the native live streaming platform on top of preparing the presentation itself—she felt that the chances were too high that something would go awry. She didn't feel she would be able to guarantee an excellent experience for attendees. She declined the invitation, explaining her reasoning and expressing her hope that, once she had more experience with the platform and as an attendee at similarly managed events, she might be considered for a future iteration of that event.

Make Your Provisional Decision

If the opportunity seems like a good fit for all the factors we've discussed so far—i.e., a good fit with your goals for yourself, your goals for your audience, and the organizer's goals—a final assessment will be a cost-benefit consideration for the specific opportunity. You must weigh any costs—financial and otherwise—you will incur against the benefits you will gain from the engagement.

Many of those costs will be related to travel, and we cover those in the section on "The Speaker on the Road," but don't forget to factor in your time investment. It's easy to fall into the trap of thinking of our time as "free," but you need to attach value to your time, whether in terms of dollars or in terms of other things you might be doing with that time—writing your next book, for example. And be sure to factor in the time spent not just at the event itself, but on all the prep and follow-up work needed to make it a success. Finally, if you have a day job and need to take time off to participate in an event, this will come either from a pool of personal time off or as unpaid time off; this needs to be factored into your cost/benefit analysis as well.

You may be in a position where your decision depends on the agreement you can negotiate with the organizer, and we delve into that in detail in the section on "Setting Your Fee and Negotiating the Offer."

Finally, you may be approached to speak at events that objectively seem desirable but that you have no passion for. Does the idea of accepting the offer leave you energized or enervated? Michael's rule of thumb is that he can tell if an event is a "zero or a hero" within two minutes of reading the organizer's email and visiting the event's website.

For example, he once received an invitation to speak at an event where the majority of the event's audience were traditionally published authors. The organizer, a forward thinker and self-publishing advocate, wanted him to speak about self-publishing but admitted that it would be a tough sell. Michael weighed the potential benefit he could provide to the audience, his time away from home, and the opportunities such an event could lead him to. He quickly determined that the answer was a definite no. He passed on the event and referred the organizer to another speaker.

Once you've decided whether or not to accept the engagement, let the organizers know promptly. Don't be like that dreaded dinner guest who waits until the last minute to RSVP in the hope that a better offer will come along. Organizers are juggling the involvement of their speakers along with many other details of an event—don't leave them hanging.

If you decide to decline the engagement, share the reasons behind your decision as appropriate. For example, if you decline because their offer includes only two nights of lodgings, but you would need three due to logistical considerations, let them know that; they might adjust their offer. If you must decline because of another commitment, let them know that and express interest in being considered for future events.

Speaker's Notes

Capture your responses to the questions below in the downloadable document available at https://www.theindyauthor.com/from-page-to-platform.html.

- What criteria will you use to assess your speaking opportunities?
- What is an example of a circumstance that would make you decide that a potential engagement was a zero, not a hero?

SETTING YOUR FEE AND NEGOTIATING THE OFFER

What to Charge

We're wholeheartedly behind the goal of having your speaking engagements be a source of direct income. In fact, we believe that money incentivizes speakers to do their best work. Furthermore, we've found that events that pay their speakers are simply better events. A budget for speakers often also means a budget for a better venue, better promotion of the event, more resources to organize the event, and so on.

There are some speakers who make a comfortable living doing speaking engagements, but they are the exception, not the rule. Most of us need to think of paid engagements as one of multiple streams of income of our author business. This will keep your expectations healthier.

If you've decided to charge for an engagement, the next question is, how much? As much as we would love to give you a formula where you could simply input some data and output a figure, we cannot. The right amount to charge depends on many factors, including:

- the venue
- the organizer's budget
- your topic
- your credibility and expertise as an author
- your credibility and expertise as a speaker
- whether other speakers at the event are being compensated (and have been compensated in the past)
- how badly the organizer needs you
- your negotiation skills

When determining what to charge for your speaking engagements, you are beholden to market forces. If you decide that you want several thousand dollars for every speaking engagement, you are pricing yourself out of range of many potential engagements that might bring you benefits other than direct income. Not only that, but organizers talk, and if you're demanding unreasonable rates, you'll develop a bad reputation.

On the other hand, when you negotiate fair deals, you not only increase your direct income but also benefit from a reputation as a professional speaker who understands the economic realities that organizers face.

If you approach an organizer about an engagement, your pitch should make your expectation of compensation clear at a high level—for example, *I look forward to discussing the terms of the engagement with you*. You don't want to engage the organizer in discussion and only at the end mention that you expect to be paid. You don't need to name a number right off the bat, but you should let them know if you're not willing to do pro bono engagements.

If you approach an organizer and don't specify the terms

as part of your pitch, then you don't have much leverage after they accept your offer. In a sense, they are doing you a favor by accepting your offer—you don't want to ask them for more.

If you are approached by an organizer, you shouldn't leave the topic of payment unaddressed for too long, but you should first get some information from the organizer about their expectations, the event, the venue, and so on, since that might influence your requirements. They may tell you that they have no money to pay you, but if the event is one you wanted to attend anyway, you don't want to have eliminated that opportunity by presenting payment as a requirement.

Also consider that money isn't the only aspect of an engagement that you can negotiate. In fact, if money is the only thing you focus on in your negotiation, you may come across as mercenary and unprofessional.

Below, we cover how you can increase your chances of negotiating a successful offer in a way that best meets all stakeholders' needs and that maintains your professionalism.

If the Offer Doesn't Include Payment

If an organizer offers you an engagement but does not offer money, and if earning direct income is a primary goal, reply this way: "I would love to speak at your event, but I typically receive X dollars for this type of engagement." See what they say—to paraphrase Wayne Gretzky, you miss one hundred percent of the shots you don't take. If they say they don't plan to pay the speakers at the event and that's a make-or-break consideration for you, don't waste their time or yours: thank them for the offer but let them know you're not able to accept.

If they show a willingness to adjust their approach in order to pay you for the engagement, and if they ask you for a number, have a target quote ready and see how they respond. If they don't respond to your email, then you've insulted them; take note of that for future negotiations. If they do respond but politely decline, then your offer was too high; that will be your lesson learned. If they accept, congratulations!

However, what will happen most of the time is that they will make a counteroffer, which will open up the negotiation. Throughout any negotiation, remember our mantra: professionalism (which includes good manners) is everything.

If the organizer can't meet your target speaker fee, consider whether accepting the engagement will repay you in other ways. Some events are worth attending because of who you might meet. Michael and Matty have both attended conferences where connections led to business opportunities. In fact, the idea for this book was born over dinner at the Writer's Digest conference at which we were speaking.

Just because an organizer can't pay you a fee doesn't mean that you can't leverage the event to earn indirect income from the event or find opportunities to further your author career. Those other opportunities might make the time and money you will invest in participating in the event worthwhile.

If the Offer Does Include Payment

If an organizer approaches you with an offer that includes payment, you have a significant advantage in the negotiations since the power dynamic is that they need you more than you need them.

Fees for speakers, except for the most well-established, are more often driven by the budget of the event than by some standard fee schedule of the speaker. Therefore, we recommend against publishing your target rates because it limits your negotiating position, both in requesting a higher fee from an organizer with a generous budget and in lowering a fee for an organizer for whom you want to make a financial accommodation.

If you receive an offer that meets your speaking fee target, congratulations! Sign the contract and start your prep. (You might consider slightly increasing your target fee for similar events in the future.)

If you receive an offer that is dramatically below your target—for example, your target fee is $1,000 and they offer $50—decline it. Don't waste time haggling about a fee they will never be able to pay.

However, if you receive an offer that is comparable to but below your target, you may have room for negotiation. Say, "I would love to speak at your event, and I appreciate your offer of $X. I usually only do these events for $Y." If they offer $100, then ask for $150 or $175. If they offer $1,000, counter with $1,200 or $1,300. (You can also use this approach if the organizer meets your target fee but you feel there may be more room for negotiation.) See the section on "Negotiating Basics" for more information.

They may stand by their initial offer. You might think, "But I'm worth more than that! Shouldn't I be compensated appropriately for my speaking?" Yes, but the organizer's budget is what it is. If you want to command a higher fee, then go for it, but if you develop a reputation for being the speaker who demands unreasonably high compensation, that will hurt your reputation and reduce your chances for future engagements. We recommend that you accept the stated offer, as long as it falls within the parameters you've established for accepting an engagement.

Speakers who accept whatever fee the organizer proposes may leave some money on the table, and organizers recognize that negotiation with professional speakers is part of the process. When negotiating, be polite, respectful, and direct. Listen to the organizer's concerns and look for ways to address them. Make sure you share your concerns to give them a chance to address those.

Negotiations end one of two ways: with a deal or without a deal. Whether your negotiation results in an acceptance or a decline, end on a positive note and thank the organizer for their time and effort.

Consider Copyright

The content of your speaking engagements is your intellectual property, and as such constitutes a great part of the value you offer as a professional speaker. In our experience, most speaker agreements do not contain anything about the copyright to your talk, which is a benefit to you as a speaker since the rights will rest with you by default. If the agreement doesn't mention copyright, don't raise it as an issue with the organizer.

If the organizer wants the copyright to your talk, it means that they would be able to use the content in other venues, formats, and media with no requirement to compensate you. When you consider the value of your existing and potential IP related to your talk, the dangers of signing away copyright to your talk is clear.

Except in extraordinary circumstances, if you do grant copyright to an organizer for your talk, it should be for that specific talk at that specific venue, not your ability to give the talk in general. For example, your talk at Venue A is one piece of intellectual property; your talk at Venue B is another. This shouldn't impact your ability to give the talk at Venue C. There are some exceptions, but this is generally the case.

Also keep in mind that your engagement includes not only the talk itself but also supplemental material such as slides, handouts, bibliographies, and resource pages. Each of these elements constitutes your intellectual property and is protected by copyright. You need to carefully weigh the costs and benefits of giving up rights to any of this IP to an event organizer. If you decide to grant an organizer rights to the supplemental materials, make sure that what they can and can't do with these materials is clearly specified in the contract.

For example, Michael once spoke at an event where the organizer took the copyright to the audio, video, and supplemental materials. Michael wanted to give this talk in the future at other venues, so he negotiated the grant of rights to clarify that the organizer received the rights to the audio and video of the talk on the day of the event, but that the rights to the presentation and other supplemental materials remained with Michael. He provided the organizer with a non-exclusive license to use the presentation for the purposes of distributing the talk only. This way, both the organizer and Michael achieved their objectives with mutual benefit.

Note that if the organizer records audio or video of your talk, they own the copyright to that recording; you cannot use it without their permission. Don't upload your talk to YouTube unless the organizer gives you permission to do so. However, if the organizer allows *you* to record audio and/or video of your talk, you can use that however you want (although it's a good idea to bake this into your contract). Michael once recorded a talk on Zoom that he wanted to post on his YouTube channel. The organizer gave him permission to use it in this way as long as he waited at least 60 days after the event to do so. Michael negotiated this into the speaker's agreement so that everyone was on the same page.

We offer these cautions not only as a guard against the few but inevitable unscrupulous players out there but also because some speaker agreements are poorly drafted and can take more rights than the organizer needs or even intends. It's up to you to be vigilant to make sure that an organizer's well-intentioned (or ill-intentioned) efforts don't restrict your rights to your own IP without careful consideration.

Negotiation Basics

These guidelines will stand you in good stead in any negotiation, whether for a speaking engagement or not.

- If the event doesn't work with your schedule or doesn't align with your goals, say no quickly.
- Understand upfront what your "lines in the sand" are. Address any issues that are deal-breakers early in the process. For example, if having the organizer cover your travel expenses is a requirement for you, let them know that upfront.
- Keep your requests professional and succinct.
- Be direct—don't leave anything to interpretation. For example, don't assume that the organizer is covering your hotel just because they're paying for your flight.
- Don't encumber the process by spending time on low-value considerations. If you're driving to an engagement and the organizer is reimbursing you for mileage, don't press them to cover tolls as well.

- Don't loop back to earlier points in the negotiation. For example, once you've agreed that the organizer will pay for your airfare and lodgings, don't later return to a discussion of travel expenses to request rental car coverage.
- Don't get into a bidding war. Organizers don't like back and forth. If you can't get them to where you want them after your first counteroffer, ask yourself whether it's worth continuing.
- Respect the organizer's time—don't get to the final stages of negotiation and then bow out. (If you've assessed the opportunity carefully, this shouldn't be an issue.)
- Capture your agreement in writing. Relying on oral negotiations leaves you open to misunderstandings and possible deception. You can discuss the details of the agreement in whatever venue works best for you and the organizer, but you *must* capture the final agreement in writing.
- Make sure the talk you can deliver is commensurate with what you are asking for in the negotiation. If you want $5,000 to deliver a keynote address, you'd better be prepared to deliver $5,000 of value to the organizer and the audience.
- Don't be a jerk.

Once you've settled on the offer, stick with it. Remember, professionalism is everything.

Speaker's Notes

Capture your responses to the questions below in the downloadable document available at https://www.theindyauthor.com/from-page-to-platform.html.

- What is your target fee for each type of talk and each of your topics?
- Under what circumstances might you decide to forego a financial payment for some other benefit?

PREPARING YOUR TALK

Slides

Not all talks require slides. However, they are such a key part of many talks and, when they are used, inform so many other parts of the process of preparing a talk that we have included them first in this section.

The requirement for slides differs based on the type of talk you are giving. For example, slides are generally expected at a talk at a conference breakout session, but not necessarily for a keynote presentation. They may or may not be appropriate to support a workshop but are almost never used for panel discussions or author readings. If the use of slides for the type of talk you will be giving is optional, how do you decide whether to use them?

These factors might steer you away from using slides:

- If the venue is an intimate one—for example, a workshop of half a dozen participants—then use of slides is more likely to create a barrier between

you and your audience than to support your message.
- If your role is to focus attention on others, as would be the case when acting as master of ceremonies for an event or when moderating a panel, slides are probably more distracting than helpful.
- If you're so proficient in your topic and so dynamic a speaker that visuals are not necessary, then by all means, forgo the slides. (Only a few of the most experienced speakers can pull this off.)

For situations not falling into those categories, here are some other considerations:

- Well-designed slides can provide visual interest for participants and accommodate audience members who have a visual learning style.
- If your presentation or talk involves data or statistics, your audience will be able to absorb this information more easily via slides than via a verbal recitation.
- Slides can help alleviate speaker nervousness about being the sole focus of an audience's attention. After all, if the audience is looking at a slide, they're not looking at you. However, don't rely on your slides to hold your audience's attention; that's your responsibility as the speaker. Matty once attended a talk on Jack the Ripper, complete with photos of the Ripper's victims. Although the photos were certainly attention-getting, it was the speaker's information and presentation style that kept the audience riveted.

- Slides can provide information to prompt you through the course of your talk, but make sure you use them as prompts and not as scripts. Your audience can read slides as well as you can—they want something more from you as the speaker. Slides should support what you have to say, not replace it.

The slides you use to accompany your talk can support and reinforce your message or can cause your audience to turn to their phones and social media feeds. If you've decided that your talk and your audience would benefit from slides, this section will provide some best practices you can apply. The information we share related is program agnostic; it applies equally to Microsoft PowerPoint, Apple Keynote, Google Slides, or any other program you use to create your slides.

Establishing Your Slide Template

We start with a discussion of your slide template rather than content because it's convenient to have a template to capture your thoughts as you develop the content, and inconvenient to have to adjust the layout after you've populated the content. Furthermore, a well-chosen design can encourage you to keep your slide content minimal and not clutter it with too much verbiage.

You might be tempted to dive in and build your slides from scratch, to use one of the templates provided by your presentation software, or to download a free template. We don't recommend those approaches.

Starting from scratch can be extraordinarily time-consuming, and time you spend on this is time not spent on refining your content. Furthermore, visual design is a specialized area of expertise, and it's best to rely on professionals so that you can free yourself to focus on your own expertise: the topic of your talk.

So why not use one of the templates available through your presentation software, such as PowerPoint or Apple Keynote? Because chances are high that another speaker at the event will use the same one. Just as it would be awkward to show up at a cocktail party in the same outfit as another guest, it's awkward to have your presentation "dressed in the same outfit" as another speaker's presentation. If you do use one of the built-in templates available through your presentation software, at least steer away from the templates that the software displays first, because they will be the most heavily used.

The free downloadable templates that are available online bring a different set of challenges. The fine print for use of these templates can include terms such as the requirement to credit the creator in the slide deck. Others state that you can only use the slides for personal use. If you are giving a talk, it is commercial use even if you're not being paid for the engagement. This is especially a concern if your presentation will be recorded and distributed online. Artificial intelligence applications crawl the web searching for cases of copyright infringement. Don't take the risk.

Our recommendation? Purchase a premium slide deck template from a reputable stock media company—just search online for "premium slide presentations," and you'll find a vast number from which to choose. You'll still need to fill in your own content, but the design will be done for you. When you purchase a premium template, you can use it for commercial use, usually without any limitation or the need to give attribution.

Using a premium template will ensure that the look—the background, fonts, colors, and other style elements—is consistent throughout the presentation. At the same time, most premium templates also provide you with the flexibility to personalize them—for example by using your brand colors and logo. Michael purchases a premium slide deck every few years and customizes it with his brand colors and personal aesthetic, and the change keeps his brand look from getting stale.

A final note about selecting a template: many templates are quite elaborate, with elements like color gradient backgrounds and visual embellishments. However, there can be downsides to these details. Insufficient contrast between the background color and text color can make the text difficult to read, especially with the less powerful projectors you will encounter in some venues. Printing slides with colorful or elaborate backgrounds is quite toner intensive. And if an organizer provides a slide template they want you to use for their event, it can be tricky and time-consuming to transfer your material into the organizer's template. For this reason, Matty likes to use templates that include designer-selected elements such as font styles and text placement, but to remove the template's background elements to provide a plain background.

Creating Your Slide Content

Start working on your slides as soon as you sign your speaker's agreement, even if the talk is months away. Your presentation is likely to consume most of your preparation time, and procrastinating will just increase your stress. In addition, even though you may think you know the visuals you want to display for your audience, the act of committing content to slides often gives you a different perspective on your material. You want plenty of time to be able to assess and adjust your slides for the best experience for you and your audience.

Having your slides done in advance is a sign of professionalism; don't be that speaker who is still fiddling with slides hours (or minutes) before their talk. (At the same time, beware of Parkinson's Law, which holds that work will expand to fill the time allotted for its completion, so although you want to start your work on your presentation as soon as you sign your speaker's agreement, you need to budget your time so you don't over-engineer your presentation.)

As the expert in your topic, you are the person best equipped to determine the content that will support your goals for your presentation, but in this section, we describe a few components that every presentation should include.

Master Slide

Most presentation software will give you the option of putting key information on a master slide so that you don't have to place it individually on each slide. Think of this as the "footer" for your slides—the information should be minimal. For example, you might want to include a small version of your brand logo, your website URL, or slide numbers.

Leave room to brand the presentation appropriately for the venue. For example, Matty's presentation master for talks about the writing craft or the publishing voyage might include The Indy Author logo in one corner, with the opposite corner of the master slides left blank to accommodate the logo of the presentation host or event.

Title Slide

At a minimum, the title slide should include the title and subtitle of your presentation and your author and/or business name, but you might also include an image or design that will set the tone for your talk. Speaking on your Appalachian Trail through hike? Include a photo of you at the terminus. Speaking on authoring romance novels? Set the tone with romance-oriented images, colors, and fonts.

About Slide

The about slide will establish your credibility by providing information about you that illustrates why you are qualified to speak on the topic. It can also serve to build rapport with the audience by allowing them to get to know you as an individual. At a minimum, the about slide should contain a high-level summary of your experience and the same headshot that you provided to the organizer. Having your photo on the about slide will remind attendees of who you are if they review the presentation later and will act as an introduction to people who might not have seen your talk but might encounter your slide deck.

Other ideas for an engaging about slide include:

- an inspirational quote that you have permission to use
- a fun fact
- photographs of you and/or your family, your travels, or anything related to your expertise
- the book cover of the title you are promoting, or some of your best book covers

Use the time the slide is displayed to build rapport with your audience. You might tell a funny story related to your topic. Be creative with the about slide—it's prime real estate.

Body

What you put in the body of your slide deck will be based on your topic, your audience, and your goals. We can't provide specifics about what it should include, beyond advising you to consider the time-tested mantra of education: tell them what you are going to teach them, tell them why it is important, teach them, tell them what you taught them, and tell them what to do next.

In this section, we provide some guidelines and best practices to ensure your presentation achieves its desired goals.

Text

- Less is (usually) more. Text-heavy slides are hard to read, and if your audience wanted to read about your topic, they would have bought a book, not attended your talk.
- Less is (sometimes) less. If halving the amount of text you put on each slide means you have twice as many slides to click through, that can be distracting to your audience. (If you're breaking text across slides to keep audience members from reading ahead, use the presentation program's animation feature, where each click reveals one bulleted item or other element at a time.)
- Use bullet points to convey textual information, since they will be easier for your audience to read and will keep you from reading long passages of text from the slides. Wordsmith out any extraneous text.
- Use a consistent and brand-right font throughout. If you copy and paste text into your slides from another source, use the program's "special paste" function or the format painter tool to match the font, text size, and color of your template.
- Don't get fancy with fonts. When in doubt, use Times New Roman, Calibri, or Arial. This is especially true if you will be running the slides from a computer other than your own, since not all computers will properly display all fonts, and the computer's substitute fonts may distort the slide layout.

- Size matters. A font size of 14 or 16 is large enough to be easily readable in most presentation venues, even in large rooms where participants may be seated far from the screen, while avoiding the shouty look of overly large text.
- Avoid italics, which are difficult to read in a presentation format. Use bold instead.
- Ensure consistency of style, especially within lists. For example, if you add a period to the end of items in a bulleted list, add a period at the end of every bullet point. If most of the items in a list are a verb-noun combination (for example, *Enlist supporters*), make sure every item follows this format.

Images and Color

- As with text, less is (usually) more with images as well. Image-heavy slides look busy and distract your audience from your message.
- Stock photos are great additions to a slide deck. You can purchase them at low cost, and they will protect you from committing copyright infringement. Search online for "stock photos" and read the terms of service of any site you purchase photos from. Do not download random images directly from the Internet. You must have the rights to use every image in your presentation, and that license must be for commercial use.
- Consider using photos you've taken. They can be a great way to add character to your presentation and build rapport with the audience.

- Use SmartArt, but sparingly. SmartArt is a built-in feature with Microsoft Office products that lets you build custom and dynamic tables, graphs, and charts to present your message in a more visually compelling way. Because the feature is so easy to use, it's often overused, but it can be an effective way to underscore your talking points. You can make the use of Smart Art more seamless by matching the colors of the SmartArt with the colors of your slide template.
- Compress photos before incorporating them into your slides, especially if you have purchased high-resolution stock images for your presentation; this will keep your file size manageable and avoid logistical headaches. You can use free JPEG compression software online to reduce the file size of your images. (If the size of your presentation file is still too large to email, you can create a ZIP file to send or can upload the presentation to a cloud storage website such as Google Drive or Dropbox and share a link to the file with the organizer.)
- Make sure any color elements you add for a particular presentation are compatible with any brand colors incorporated into your slide template.
- Avoid the following color combinations, which make material less readable for people with color blindness: red and green, blue and purple, green and brown, red and brown. Do some web research to find colorblind-friendly palettes.
- Use the alignment and centering tools when

adding elements to make your slides pleasing to the eye.

Video, Audio, and Animation

Because technical issues arise all too frequently with audio, video, and animation in presentations, we recommend avoiding them unless they are intrinsic to your presentation (e.g., a presentation on identifying bird songs will be far more compelling with audio).

- If you must use audio or video, don't try to embed it in your presentation software. Instead, click out of your presentation software to an audio or video player and then return to the slide deck after you've played the audio or video.
- If you must use audio, be sure to test how audible it is in the actual presentation space with the actual presentation equipment. Audio that sounds fine in your home office might be completely unintelligible in a large ballroom.
- Use animations sparingly. They can grab an audience's attention, but overuse is distracting. In fact, organizers may remove them. Michael once spoke at an engagement where the organizer removed his animations because they planned to publish a replay of the talk, and removing the animations made it easier to edit the video in postproduction.

External Sources

Whenever possible, keep everything you need to access local to the presentation computer. Trying to access external sources such as websites introduces all sorts of opportunities for technical issues, especially if you are using the venue's computer, which may have unexpected restrictions on what sites or information it can access. The strength of the venue's Wi-Fi is another variable and is often outside the organizer's control.

Recap Slide

If your content is complex, consider using a recap slide that gathers the big ideas on one slide for participants to see, and perhaps to print out for later reference.

The Final Slide: The Call to Action (CTA)

The call to action (CTA) is the pitch you make to the participants at the end of your talk or presentation. Although you may have a CTA based on the content of your presentation—for example, "If I've convinced you of the importance of exercise, will you commit to scheduling 10 minutes of exercise a day starting tomorrow?"—the CTA we're addressing here is the call for the audience to engage with you beyond the talk.

Your CTA might be, "If you enjoyed this presentation, please check out my book ..." or "For more advice on this topic, contact me at ..." Your CTA slide supports this message. Consider including a QR code that participants can scan from their seats and that will take them to an appropriate online site.

If you include a QR code, make it as big as possible so that audience members can scan it from their seats. Also share the code's URL for those who don't know how QR codes work.

What you verbalize to your audience should be a soft sell, but what you present on the slide can be an overt pitch. If you're promoting one of your books, include the book cover, a QR code link to the book, and any other information that will entice your audience to purchase the book and that will make it easy for them to find it. This is your best chance to get people to take action, so don't be shy, but don't be pushy either.

A good rule of thumb for striking the right balance in your CTA slide is to assess it first as a participant and then as an organizer sitting in on the presentation. The participant should be intrigued and should have all the information they need to find the pitched resource. The organizer should feel comfortable that you're not making a hard sell. Organizers *hate* hard sells—their event will lose credibility and gain an undesirable reputation if its speakers hassle participants to spend their money—so keep your selling soft!

We recommend that your CTA slide be your final slide, and that you keep it up for the remainder of the time you're on the podium. Don't click away from this slide to an "empty" closing slide such as *Questions?* or *Thank you!* that provides no benefit to either you or your audience.

Putting It All Together

If you follow the advice in this section, you will ensure that your slides will support and not hinder conveying your message successfully, and that your audience will leave your talk wanting to continue to engage with you and your resources.

Generally, it takes two or three drafts before most presentations settle into their final form. After that, you'll find that the changes you make are minimal. (If you're still fiddling with the details, ask yourself if you might be over-engineering.)

Even if you're delivering a presentation you've given before, review your slides in advance for opportunities to apply what you've learned about yourself, your topic, and your audience since the last presentation.

Your Presentation Library

When you're first starting your speaker career, the

creation of material—often slides—to support your message may be the most time-consuming part of prepping for an engagement. As your speaking engagements increase, if you continue to approach every presentation as a blank slate, then it will continue to be the most time-consuming part. This blank slate approach has obvious negatives for you as the speaker since you never enjoy any efficiency benefits. But it also has negatives for your audience, since they are less likely to benefit from refinements you make from one talk to another.

The solution for optimizing the experience for you and your audience is to develop a presentation library.

Stock your presentation library with a master presentation for each topic for which you want to pitch yourself as a speaker. Capture everything you might want to include in a talk in that master. Once you have that master presentation, you can then pull from it what is appropriate for a particular engagement.

For example, Matty has a master presentation titled *Podcasting*, containing slides covering everything she knows on that topic. From that, she could pull material for talks focused on more specific podcasting-related topics: *What Podcast Format is Right for You?* or *Landing a Podcast Guest Spot* or *Best Tech for Starting a Podcast*.

After your talk, review the master from which you pulled it and incorporate any learnings you had from your presentation. Did the audience seem confused by one of the slides? Clarify the text. Did they squint to read information? Make the font bigger. By making these improvements in the master presentation, every subsequent presentation you pull from it will benefit.

Notes

Even some of the most experienced speakers use notes during their talks, but this material should be brief written prompts to remind you of key points, not a script from which you read. Using a newspaper analogy, the content of the notes should be the headlines, not the articles. Consider the best format to use to achieve this goal.

Presentation applications often include a feature that enables you to record notes that are visible only to you, not your audience, and these can be a valuable place to capture thoughts as you're developing your slides. However, using them during the presentation itself can be problematic. First, it can lure you in to speaking to your computer monitor, not to your audience. Second, depending on the tech set-up of the venue, you may not be able to see the in-program speaker notes in the same way you see them in your practice sessions on your computer—for example, if you're given a remote to use to click through the slides.

Paper notes have the benefit of not being subject to the vagaries of technical glitches, but don't use them as a prop, and definitely don't hold them during your talk. You should be able to glance quickly at your notes on the lectern, collect your thoughts, and then step away from your notes to deliver the next section of your talk. Make sure the font of your notes is big enough that you can read them easily at a glance.

Matty recommends printing out your notes on card stock rather than normal printer paper since it's easier to handle and more durable. Be sure to number the pages in case they get out of order.

Handouts

Handouts may seem like an outmoded concept, but they can serve two important functions:

- To convey information included in your talk
- To market you, your expertise, and your offerings

The use of handouts to convey information is especially important if you have a complex or highly data-dependent topic. You might include graphs or other illustrations that support your information, and having this in handout form enables attendees to spend more time on it even after you've advanced to another slide. Handouts are also a boon to attendees who might have trouble seeing information on the screen.

If you believe slides will be beneficial to your audience to better convey the information you want to share, consider the format you want to use. Presentation software usually has the option of printing out slides in handout form, with multiple slides per sheet. This is usually not the best option. Not only is it a highly inefficient use of paper, but if your slides don't have a plain white background, it's also a highly inefficient use of printer ink. Slide layouts are optimized for viewing on a screen; you need to modify information for handouts to optimize for reading up close.

Consider if there's a way you can condense the information you want attendees to take from your talk onto a few pages. This is not only an efficient use of paper, but if your handout is pleasingly formatted and the information on it is compelling, attendees might save it for ongoing reference.

Matty has such a handout for a talk she gives on independent publishing titled "Indie Publishing in a Nutshell"; it graphically represents the production and distribution options indie authors have for ebook, print, and audio, one format per page of the handout.

An effective handout is not only a service to the people you want to reach but can also act as a powerful marketing tool for the products or services you have to offer.

What should you include in the handout to support its use as a marketing tool?

- reiterations of key content on your slides, such as facts, figures, images, and charts
- a QR code that links to a page on your website
- a direct link to your website - If you have created an event-specific page, link to that, or to a page that features a book you're promoting that's related to the topic of your talk.
- a special offer
- bibliographies and other reference materials

Look for opportunities to make your handout available even to event attendees who didn't attend your talk.

- If the room is small enough, put a copy of the handout on each chair ahead of your talk.
- Put extra copies on a table near the door to the room where your talk is held so that as attendees enter and leave, they can pick up an extra copy should they desire.
- Find out if the organizers have a central location where more copies of handouts can be left. (If you can do this ahead of your talk, it can be a great way to increase attendance.)

- If the organizers allow it, put a downloadable file on your website event page. You can offer to disable the page a few days after the event so that it won't be readily available to non-attendees.

Many speakers don't bother with handouts, or they take the easy way out and just print out their slides in handout format. A carefully planned and designed handout will better serve your audience, and better serve you as they use it as a tool to remind them of your talk, sometimes long after it has taken place.

If you've assembled the material you want to include in your handout but aren't sure how to present it, consider hiring a design professional on a freelancer platform.

Practice, Practice, Practice

Once you've constructed your presentation, you need to practice it. A prepared speaker is a relaxed speaker. A relaxed speaker puts the audience at ease, which makes it easier for them to receive the message and heed your call to action. Prepared speakers also put organizers at ease. There is no better recipe for success than adequate preparation—it's what separates the pros from the amateurs.

Practicing will allow you to refine the content, flow, cadence, physicality, and timing of your talk. A rule of thumb is that for every hour of presentation, you should spend at least three hours of practice when you are initially refining it. As you become more familiar with the material, you can reduce the practice time a bit—but never reduce it to zero.

Create a Realistic Practice Environment

If you plan to use notes for your presentation, you must practice your delivery so that your notes do not impede your message. The audience must not be distracted by you referencing your notes. If you don't plan to use notes, you must prepare thoroughly enough that you do not meander, but you can't prepare so much that you're robotic.

Practice in an environment as similar as possible to the one in which you will be presenting. For example, if you will be standing behind a lectern with a presentation remote, do your best to replicate that situation. If you will be moving back and forth on a stage with no lectern, replicate that situation. Don't practice sitting down (unless you're in the unusual situation of having to present while seated). If you're using slides, practice with the slides. If you are using some other materials or props, use those during your practice. Speaking the content aloud will help you identify stumbling areas such as tongue twisters.

Be Your Own Audience

Make a video recording of your practice sessions for your review. This is not only a great way to assess your performance but watching it a few times will further familiarize you with the presentation content and organization, which will reduce your reliance on your notes.

Pay attention to your posture, tone, physical presence, and how you move. Be aware of habitual gestures that might be distracting. Matty tends to flap her hands penguin-style. Michael suffers from the "ping pong" problem—he tends to pace around the stage and has been known to walk so fast that cameras can't keep up with him in recorded sessions. This is where making a video of your practice session can be especially revealing. In fact, it's sometimes easier to pick out these physical tics if you watch the video at double speed.

Watch out for filler words like *um, uh,* and *you know,* which slow down the delivery of your content. Being aware of these verbal tics is the first step to eliminating them. If you're using filler words to give yourself time to collect your thoughts, use silence instead. If you're using filler words because you're talking quickly—picking up extra words like a snowball picking up mass as it rolls downhill—slow down.

If there are one or possibly two lessons you've gleaned from your review of your practice session videos that you believe you might forget during your actual talk, consider attaching small sticky notes to your computer as reminders. These should be one-word reminders: *Smile!* or *Breathe!* Anything more than that will be more distracting than helpful.

Hit the Marks

Delivering your talk out loud is the only way you will be able to judge how long it will take. Set a stopwatch and don't look at it until you've completed your practice run. Then assess if you need to adjust to meet the time requirements set by the organizer, being sure to leave time for questions and answers. Make the needed adjustments, then run through the talk again.

Once you've achieved your target timing, mark in your notes the approximate quarter, half, and three-quarters marks so that you can gauge your progress through the presentation during the actual event. This will help you adjust on the fly since, no matter how carefully you prepare and practice, it's difficult to know exactly how long your talk will last when you deliver it in front of an audience. If you're a bit nervous, you might talk faster. If the audience doesn't have as much knowledge about the topic as you assumed, you may have to slow down or take time to provide additional information. But despite this, you still need to complete the talk in the time allocated to you.

How do you make these adjustments on the fly?

To accommodate a situation where you're progressing

through the presentation more slowly than expected, identify those topics or slides that you can skip over or abbreviate without significantly impacting the message or information you want to convey. You might mark these in your notes, or even on the slide itself, perhaps with a subtle icon whose significance only you will know. For example, in Matty's presentations on podcasting for authors, she usually includes a slide with a list of inexpensive options for podcasting tech. If her talk is running as scheduled, she'll review each of these items. If the talk is running behind, she can direct audience members to her website, where they will find this information as well as additional detail.

To accommodate a situation where you're progressing through the presentation more quickly than expected, have a slide or two at the end related to your topic that you can share optionally. For example, in Matty's presentation "Publishing Tips for the Frugal Author: Getting the Most for Your Editing and Design Dollars," she has a slide titled "Other Frugal Tips" that includes items not related to editing or design—for example, the value of buying ISBNs in bulk. She can skip this slide without lessening the message of the presentation but can tap into it if needed to fill the presentation time, providing even more value to her audience.

Enlist a Practice Audience

Once you feel comfortable giving your talk to yourself—in the mirror or via video recording—you'll want to recruit an audience for your practice. You can join a public speaking-focused organization like Toastmasters International to hone your general presentation skills, but to practice a specific presentation, you'll want to recruit a good-natured volunteer who is as similar to your intended audience as possible. (Bonus points if they also have experience as a speaker.)

Giving your talk to a practice audience is vital for

assessing content and flow. It's difficult for a speaker to assess for themselves aspects like whether the level of detail the talk includes is appropriate, whether the speed at which they are moving through the material is optimal, or whether supporting material like visuals or a handout is or would be helpful in conveying their message. With a practice audience, you can not only rely on their explicit input on these factors, but you can also watch out for expressions of confusion or surprise.

Your practice audience can also help you identify concepts, verbiage, or images that might raise objections from the audience. We're not saying you should necessarily eliminate these—you need to make that decision based on your content and your goals for yourself and your audience—but you need to be prepared to address these objections.

Watch for signs that you need to adjust the cadence of your talk. Your audience will come to your talk because you know more about the topic than they do, and you need to deliver the information in a cadence that gives them time to absorb and even reflect on what you're saying. As you come to the end of a section, pause for a moment to let them think back on what you've said. If you pose a question that you want the audience to consider, make sure to give them time to do so (and be explicit about whether you want them to consider it silently or are soliciting active participation and want them to share their answers with you and their fellow attendees).

The goal of your practice is to get comfortable with all the aspects of your talk so you can focus on your message and on serving your audience when you get onstage.

Speaker's Notes

Capture your responses to the questions below in the downloadable document available at https://www.theindyauthor.com/from-page-to-platform.html.

- How and where will you create realistic practice environments that mimic as closely as possible the venues where you will be delivering your talk?
- From where and how will you solicit your practice audience so that they are as similar as possible to your target audience?

SELLING YOUR BOOKS

One of the benefits—in some cases, the primary goal—of obtaining speaking engagements is the opportunity to sell your books.

Your best chance of laying the groundwork for a book sale is during your talk. Ideally, you have a book that is directly tied to the topic of your talk; in fact, Michael only accepts speaking engagements on topics that are explicitly tied to one of his books. However, even if your books are not (yet) tied to the topic, your talk itself can still be a compelling enticement for your audience to buy your books. If your talk is professionally constructed and compellingly delivered, your audience should be able to expect the same from your book. (Of course, make sure the book delivers on that promise.)

How can you improve your chances of making a book sale without making your talk sound like a sales pitch?

- Unless it seems intrusive, bring a book stand and display your book on a table at the front of the room or on stage during your talk.

- If your book is directly related to the topic of your talk, as people are taking their seats before the talk begins, hand around a copy of your book with copies of your business cards inserted in the pages and invite the attendees to take a card. (Labeling the book *Display Copy* can help ensure they don't take the book itself!)
- If your talk is based on your book, mention that briefly but clearly at the beginning of the talk; if you are using slides, include an image of the cover on an introductory slide.
- Include an appropriate URL on your slides. Matty's presentations include TheIndyAuthor.com or MattyDalrymple.com in the footer, depending on whether the audience is made up of fellow authors or of potential readers of her fiction work. Having the URL on every slide means that at whatever point an attendee's interest is piqued enough to want to know more, the source for that information is immediately available to them.
- Use the last slide of your presentation—the slide you will leave up as you answer questions from the audience—to highlight your books. If one is directly tied to the topic of your talk, feature that. If there are none that are directly tied to the topic, then include images of others to establish your position as an expert in related topics. Consider adding a QR code that leads to an appropriate web page.
- Give away free bonuses that include reference and links to your book. If the attendees like the bonuses, they'll be more likely to buy your books.

In-person Events

There are three scenarios for book sales at in-person events: you may be able to sell books directly to attendees, you may enter into a consignment arrangement with the event bookseller, or the event bookseller might purchase your books from a distributor.

Direct Sales

If you will be selling books directly to attendees, one option is obviously to bring a supply of books to the event or ship them there in advance if the organizer has made the necessary logistical arrangements. However, another option is to take orders—including payments—for books that you will ship to attendees after the conference. Attendees often prefer this because of its convenience. If you pursue this approach, be sure to have a display copy of your book available for attendees to peruse.

To accommodate attendees who prefer ebooks, have cards or handouts available that include a QR code to a place where they can purchase.

Consignment

Consignment arrangements also require you to get copies of your book to the event. The bookseller sells books from your supply, then pays you a percentage of the sales and returns the unsold books to you. A 60/40 split favoring the bookseller is a common arrangement, but terms vary by seller. This type of arrangement is more common for indie-published authors than for authors published through a publishing house.

The number of books you will sell at an event will vary greatly based on factors like how many attendees will be at the event, how well known you are to the attendees, how attendees traveled to the event (attendees are less likely to buy books if they have to haul them home on a train or plane) and, of course, how impressed they were by your talk. Consult with the organizers and the bookseller about their recommendations for the number of books you should bring.

Bookseller Purchases Books from Distributor

Alternatively, conference booksellers may purchase your books from a commonly used distributor such as Ingram, which is accessible to indie authors via platforms such as IngramSpark and Draft2Digital Print.

Having the event bookseller purchase books from a distributor is convenient for you because it prevents you from having to bring a supply of books to the conference. To make this arrangement appealing to the bookseller, authors generally need to make their books returnable.

If you're an indie author, you need to be familiar with the fees associated with returns to the distribution platform you're using. To reduce the risk of hefty return fees, work with the organizer and the bookseller to set appropriate expectations for the number of books to be ordered. If you do make the books returnable, a solution for both you and the bookseller is to have an agreement ahead of time that you will purchase any unsold copies at a discounted rate.

Because of the complexities of switching between return statuses, we do not recommend switching books to returnable to accommodate a specific event and then switching them back to non-returnable afterwards.

For authors who are not independently published, the publishing house will generally manage this process and accept most or all of the financial risk.

Covering Your Bases

Even if the organizers have partnered with a bookseller for the event, consider bringing some books with you in case the bookseller sells out. They might be willing to take additional stock from you on consignment, or they and the organizers might be okay with you selling books direct in this circumstance; be sure to check with them before making any sales.

Virtual Events

Virtual events also offer the opportunity for book sales.

- At the end of your talk, be sure to give a strong call to action that tells the audience where to buy your books. Couple that with a slide that showcases the book cover and an easy-to-remember URL or QR code.
- Display your books on a shelf behind you.
- Have an image of your book cover as your virtual background or get a poster or banner to display in your actual background.
- Wear a shirt with your name or brand (e.g., *The Indy Author, Author Level Up*) so that people see that throughout the talk. (Make sure that the text is visible on video—it's no good wearing a branded shirt if you have the camera positioned tight on your face.)
- Use a graphic overlay or text banner, sometimes called "lower thirds," to display your name, the book's title, and a URL where participants can learn more.

Speaker's Notes

Capture your responses to the questions below in the downloadable document available at https://www.theindyauthor.com/from-page-to-platform.html.

- For in-person events, what steps will you take to ensure that your books are as attractive as possible to organizers, affiliated booksellers, and attendees?
- For virtual events, what steps will you take to make it easy for attendees to find and purchase your books, without making your pitch seem too salesy?

THE SPEAKER ON THE ROAD

In this section, we share some of our hard-earned lessons about the travel that is often a part of a professional speaker's career, and how you can minimize the negative impacts, both financial and personal.

Travel Costs

Travel and living expenses related to in-person events can be significant. Some of these can be negotiated as part of your speaker's fee; some cannot. In fact, trying to negotiate some of these into your agreement may incur more negatives in terms of lost goodwill than gains in terms of financial benefit. But you need to be aware of all of them so you can make an informed decision about the financial costs and benefits of accepting a speaking engagement.

Regardless of the agreement you reach with a particular organizer, make sure all terms of payment are clearly spelled out in your contract so that you can hold the organizer accountable. Also be sure to keep travel, lodging, and meal receipts since these expenses are tax deductible.

Ideally, the host pays for your travel upfront, sometimes through a travel agent, with no money out of your pocket. However, some organizers will ask you to pay for the travel and then reimburse you later. This means money out of your pocket as well as the administrative overhead of invoicing the organizer and tracking payment. If you agree to any out-of-pocket costs, do your homework to confirm that the event organizer is reputable and solvent, and that it will be able to deliver on its financial obligation to you.

Common (but never guaranteed) expenses for an organizer to cover are your travel to the event (e.g., airfare, train fare) and lodgings; if the organizer's draft contract doesn't include these, try to negotiate them in. Some other costs, listed below, are less commonly covered. We provide guidance on how flexible organizers might be about covering these, and when you should assume that you'll likely be footing the bill.

Extra Lodging

Always compare the time you need to be at the event with the organizers' coverage for lodgings. Organizers will generally pay for your hotel room the night before and after your engagement: if you're scheduled to speak on a Saturday, they'll pay for your room Friday and Saturday night, with a departure on Sunday.

However, Matty once spoke at an event where her involvement at a conference spread over three days, but the organizer's standard contract covered only two nights. This would have required Matty to travel to the venue on the day of her talk. That was problematic for two reasons: any delay might prevent her from reaching the venue in time, and even if there were no delays, she would have gone into her first talk tired from the trip. When she conveyed this to the organizers, they were happy to cover an extra night of lodging.

Rideshares, Taxis, and Ground Transportation

There may be costs for getting from an airport or train station to the venue, and sometimes even from one venue location to another. Investigate free options, such as the free shuttle service many hotels offer or getting a lift from an event volunteer. If this is not available, you may need to rely on taxis or rideshare services. These can be surprisingly pricey, especially if you need to use them during a surge pricing period. Try to negotiate this cost into your speaker fee. If the organizer declines to pay, make sure that you've factored ground transportation into your cost-benefit analysis.

Cars

If you drive your own car to an event, you might ask the organizer to pay a stipend—either a flat fee or a per mile rate. A good guideline for a per mile rate is the mileage reimbursement rate provided by your country's government at the time of your negotiation, easily searchable online.

Organizers generally won't pay for a rental car since if you get in an accident, they could be held liable. However, the biggest consideration for you to think about is breakdowns. We strongly suggest purchasing 24/7 roadside assistance from the rental car company or verifying that your personal auto insurance provides roadside assistance in the event of a breakdown. Obtaining this coverage via the rental car company or your insurance company helps ensure that you are dealing with reputable service, since most of these organizations vet their providers. (Michael has dealt with his fair share of shady tow truck drivers, and he wouldn't wish them on his worst enemies.)

A collision damage waiver for your rental car is also a smart investment. This will provide coverage for accidents or theft. Event venues provide several factors that appeal to thieves: underground garages and/or big parking lots with poor lighting populated by cars with out-of-town plates. If your rental car is damaged, rental agreements stipulate that you'll still be responsible for the damage, even if it's not your fault. You don't need this stress as a speaker. Buying the collision damage waiver will give you peace of mind that if anything happens, it won't be your problem.

Food

Organizers will generally not pay you a per diem for food or reimburse you for food you purchase and asking them to cover these expenses may brand you as unprofessional. However, many organizers do provide some complimentary food at the event: a speakers' dinner, a catered lunch, snacks, or meals already included in the cost of attending the event. Enjoy the free food and expect to pay for anything else yourself. You might also bring a small supply of snacks with you.

Meds and Sundries

It's far easier and less expensive to bring the meds and sundries you might need at an event than to take time off to try to obtain them while you're on the road. Don't be late for your talk because you're trying to track down toothpaste. This is especially true if the venue isn't near stores where these items would be available. If a venue hotel has these available, the prices will be high. Many of these items are available in travel sizes at your local pharmacy, so they don't take up much room in your luggage.

Items we recommend are:

- Prescription medicine
- Over-the-counter medicine such as pain reliever, antacid, sleep aids, eye drops, and medicines to combat allergy, diarrhea, heartburn, motion sickness, pain, fever, cough, etc. (Even if you don't have a cough, cough drops can help relieve dry mouth immediately before your talk.)

- First aid kit that includes bandages, gauze, and antiseptic ointment
- Supplies such as cotton swabs, a digital thermometer, and tweezers

Michael has assembled a kit of these items that he keeps in his luggage—he reviews the contents of the kit periodically to replace any expired items.

Travel Insurance

Despite the importance of this item, we leave a discussion of travel insurance to the end because we feel that its importance will be clearer now that you have a better idea of all the other costs that travel to your speaker engagements will involve.

Although organizers will generally not pay for travel insurance, Michael recommends you purchase it. The cost is typically between 4 percent and 12 percent of the cost of your trip; the fact that travel insurance is a tax-deductible expense reduces the sting of incurring it.

Michael has four travel insurance stories that illustrate the importance of this coverage:

- Two weeks before Michael was scheduled to go to Las Vegas with his wife, he was struck by a devastating illness and was hospitalized for a month. Because he didn't purchase travel insurance, he lost several thousand dollars.
- Two days before Michael was scheduled to go to Disney World in Orlando, Florida, on a family vacation, his grandfather passed away. Because Michael had purchased travel insurance that covered the death of a loved one, the insurer reimbursed him for the full cost of the trip—the

best one hundred dollars he ever spent. All it took was five minutes to fill out a claim on the travel insurance company's app, a quick phone call with a claims adjuster, and a week to receive payment. This was especially important because even though he bought refundable plane tickets, he was past the period to get his refund.

- During a trip to Dallas for a speaking engagement, Michael found himself stranded overnight due to an airplane maintenance issue. He had to book a hotel room for the night, pay for a rideshare for transportation to the nearest hotel, purchase an extra dinner and breakfast he didn't plan for, and pay for another rideshare to get back to the airport the next morning. This was several hundred dollars' worth of expenses, and because the fault was with the airline, there was no way the event organizer could be expected to cover these costs. (And naturally, the airline evaded all responsibility and told Michael to go fly a kite.) Fortunately, Michael had purchased travel insurance, which covered all his expenses.
- While Michael was traveling home from Saudi Arabia after an international speaking engagement, the airline lost his luggage. Fortunately, he had purchased a travel insurance policy that paid him a lump sum of $500 in the event of lost luggage. After filling out a quick claim form, Michael received the money in his bank account the next week. He was lucky that this happened on the way home—imagine if this had happened on his outbound flight!

Here are some of the things travel insurance can cover, pulled from one of Michael's travel insurance policies:

- Accidental Death and Dismemberment – If you die at your speaking engagement, the policy will pay your family a sum, similar to life insurance.
- Emergency Evacuation and Repatriation of Remains – If you must return home due to a covered emergency, the policy will pay you. Or, if you die at your event, the policy will pay money to your family to help get your body home.
- Medical Expenses – If you have an accident while at your speaking engagement and require medical treatment, the policy will pay for your treatment up to a specified amount.
- Trip Cancellation – If you must cancel your trip for a covered reason, the policy will reimburse you for your travel costs. For example, you might buy a non-refundable airline ticket and then have to cancel due to an emergency.
- Trip Delay – If your trip is delayed because of a covered reason, you'll receive a cash payment. For example, if you end up sitting on the tarmac for several hours because of a maintenance issue with the plane, the insurance company will put money into your account for the inconvenience. (This has happened to Michael several times.)
- Missed Connection – If you miss a connecting flight, the policy will pay you for the inconvenience.
- Baggage Delay – If you make it to your destination but your bags don't, the policy will pay you cash so that you can buy what you need.

- Medical expenses, including COVID coverage – This is particularly useful if you are traveling outside of your country. Some countries won't let you in unless you can prove that you have health insurance that covers COVID. Sure, you can rely on your health insurance policy, but most travel insurance policies automatically include health insurance in the cost of the policy. Health insurance in other countries can be extraordinarily expensive, especially for non-nationals. Some countries, like Mexico, require you to pay cash upfront before treatment. Michael had a colleague who traveled to Mexico on a business trip. While he was at the hotel bar, someone put Rohypnol in his cocktail. He collapsed soon after. Fortunately, the criminal didn't get a chance to rob him because he was with several friends who called an ambulance. Upon arriving at the hospital, the doctors were concerned for his safety and prepared a treatment plan—but not before requiring his wife to go to the nearest ATM to withdraw several thousand dollars. Medical accidents happen to everyone, and it doesn't matter whether they're your fault—you still must have insurance. Travel insurance can be a great way to protect yourself on international trips, though this benefit as related to medical expenses is not needed domestically.

Read the fine print to fully understand what any travel insurance you're considering will cover and purchase it immediately after you book your airfare. Some companies have cutoff periods for when you can buy a policy, so don't wait until the last minute.

Travel insurance is an important and relatively inexpensive but overlooked investment that can protect you in many ways.

Travel Tips

Here are some other tips we've gathered based on our travel experiences as author speakers.

Avoid traveling on the same day you're scheduled to speak. This not only avoids you showing up to your talk exhausted or frazzled, but also greatly reduces the impact of travel delays caused by inclement weather, cancelled flights, road closures, traffic jams, and so on.

Book your travel so as to arrive at the venue as early in the day as you can. Better to show up early to your hotel and have to wait for check-in than to schedule your travel late in the day and risk missing the last flight.

If traveling the day before your talk means incurring an additional night of lodging, ask the organizer if they will cover this; it's in their best interest that their speakers show up at the event rested, refreshed, and ready to deliver the best possible talk for the attendees.

Save all travel information on your phone in case you find yourself without cell service. This includes the organizer's contact information and the venue address.

Planes

Limiting yourself to carry-on luggage will eliminate the delays of checking your bags and the possibility that you and your bags might end up at different destinations. Ideally, use a backpack or other wheel-less bag that you can put underneath the seat in front of you. This way, you won't have to fight people for overhead bin space—or worse, have your bag relegated to courtesy checked baggage.

If you're traveling by air, put your laptop in your carry-on luggage to avoid the punishment that checked baggage endures and to ensure it reaches your destination with you.

If you do need to check bags, make sure to pack clothing in your carryon that you can use for your talk should your luggage go astray.

Consider bringing chewing gum to help deal with air pressure changes. You can even purchase a Eustachian tube exerciser that will normalize the air pressure in your ears instantly. Swabbing the insides of your nostrils with aloe vera can help ease the discomfort of the excessively dry air in airplanes.

Trains

Many trains don't have food service, and any food that is available is likely to be unappealing. Bring your own food and drink—water, sandwiches, fruit, trail mix—as well as a bag for garbage.

Even trains that claim to have Wi-Fi don't guarantee a reliable connection; make sure you have any material you need for the trip stored locally on your laptop.

Automobiles

Driving to the venue has the advantage that you can bring "just in case" items that would be awkward to deal with if you traveled by plane or train—for example:

- copies of your books to sell via consignment through an event bookstore or to sell direct if appropriate
- as much luggage and clothing as you want
- banners and other promotional materials that

would be inconvenient or expensive to ship to the venue
- toiletries larger than airport authorities' size restrictions

If you're driving your own car, make sure it's in good repair and that regularly scheduled maintenance is performed in advance of travel to reduce the chances of a breakdown. And remember to track mileage driven to and from the event since these are tax deductible.

Speaker's Notes

Capture your responses to the questions below in the downloadable document available at https://www.theindyauthor.com/from-page-to-platform.html.

- What items, such as medications, will you pack in your speaker "go bag"?

DRESSING FOR SUCCESS

The clothing you wear for your speaking events will be a key contributor to—or detractor from—your image as a professional. There's nothing that will distract your audience from the message you want to convey more than a wardrobe malfunction, and there's nothing that can distract you from conveying that message effectively more than inappropriate or uncomfortable clothing. By making informed wardrobe selections, you can ensure that the attention of you and your audience will be where you want it to be: on your talk.

Setting aside obvious exceptions, this advice applies equally to in-person or virtual events.

Match the Level of Formality to the Event and Venue

As in all aspects of a speaking engagement, comply with any guidelines the organizer provides. Factoring that in, consider what you would wear as an attendee and then notch it up slightly. Would you wear jeans as an attendee? Upgrade to something other than denim. Would you wear a sport coat as an attendee? Add a tie.

Guard against overdressing. If everyone at the event is wearing T-shirts, jeans, and sandals, you'll distance yourself from them if you're dressed for a visit to Wall Street. You want to connect with your audience and your fellow event attendees. If you are dressed much more formally than they are, you create a subconscious barrier that will make it harder to connect.

Regardless of the level of formality, always dress neatly to convey the professionalism that is such an important aspect of your speaker persona.

Be Comfortable

Don't overlook the importance of comfortable clothing. You need to focus on giving a great talk, not fussing with a too-tight waistband. You also need to be psychologically comfortable. Don't force yourself to wear bright colors if you are more comfortable in subdued hues.

How about Branded Clothing?

Clothing bearing your own logo or slogan can be a great way to convey your brand to event attendees. If you're the only person—or one of a few—who will be wearing that brand, it can be a great way to facilitate informal meetups at the event (e.g., "Just look for my Author Level Up t-shirt!"). If more people will be wearing your branded clothing, it can be a great way to identify your tribe; consider arranging a group photo on a day when everyone will be wearing their branded item.

Branded clothing can serve as a conversation starter. Matty has a drawstring bag featuring The Indy Author name and logo, and it has led to several fellow event attendees identifying themselves as listeners of The Indy Author Podcast.

(The drawstring bag has the added advantage over a branded clothing item like a shirt of being more easily readable in more scenarios.)

However, when considering whether to wear branded clothing, factor in the organizer's preferences. Organizers of a strongly branded event are probably not going to want speakers to dilute that brand by wearing a shirt with the speaker's brand. Also, since branded clothing such as T-shirts and hoodies tend to be more casual than non-branded clothing, consider the formality of the event. If in doubt, leave branding out.

Consider a Uniform

By "uniform," we mean not a military outfit but rather a standard set of clothing that meets the wardrobe requirements of most of your appearances. For example, Matty's uniform as host of The Indy Author Podcast is a collarless knit top (a neutral level of formality that never clashes with the guest's style) with three-quarter-length sleeves (appropriate for any season) and a jewel neck (high enough to be discreet, low enough to add a touch of formality). She usually wears a necklace and small pendant (another nod toward formality but not distracting, either to Matty or her guests) and small hoop earrings (no dangling earrings, which tend to click against her earbuds). The outfit is intentionally unobtrusive because she wants the attention to be on the guest.

However, if Matty is the guest on someone else's podcast, she chooses a more varied wardrobe, and one appropriate to the subject of the appearance—e.g., darker colors if she's doing an interview about her suspense, thriller, and mystery fiction, blue-toned clothes if she's discussing the writing craft and the publishing voyage using her favorite nautical metaphors.

Michael almost always wears solid color button-down Oxfords to speaking engagements. He can dress them up with a sport coat and tie or dress them down with jeans and Chucks. He owns the same shirt in every color.

You can even make your uniform part of your brand—consider Steve Jobs' black turtleneck or Anna Wintour's signature oversize sunglasses.

Before settling on your uniform, practice your talk in front of a mirror wearing those clothes so you can catch things like a slip showing when you raise your arms or a chunky bracelet that interferes with your ability to manipulate the computer mouse.

How do you decide what your uniform should be? Consider our list of best (dressed) practices below.

Best (Dressed) Practices

- Bring a watch to help you track the time during your talk—it's easier to glance quickly at a watch than to try to check the time on your phone.
- Wearing a new outfit? Check for renegade price tags!
- Add a zipper check to your last-minute appearance prep checklist.
- When choosing a top, pick a color and material that will disguise perspiration stains.
- Take a tip from on-air professionals like news anchors and stick with solid colors. Prints and patterns can be distracting, especially on video.
- Use color to support your persona and message: blue makes you appear more dependable; pink or

purple more artistic; brown, navy, and gray more business-like.
- Wrinkled clothes are a no-no. The iron in your hotel room is sufficient for most clothing types, but not sport coats or ties. Invest in a cheap clothes steamer and keep it in your suitcase. If you're in a pinch, you can also hang your clothes next to the shower and let the steam help smooth out the wrinkles. If you can spare the time and cash, consider using the hotel's dry-cleaning service or a local dry cleaner's express option. Steer away from fabrics that are intentionally wrinkled looking.
- In larger venues, the AV tech may want to outfit you with a wireless mic, and it helps to have an article of clothing to which the mic can easily be attached—for example, the back of your waistband or belt, versus a beltless dress, which doesn't provide obvious places to which to attach the mic.
- A pocket is handy for storing a tissue but in general keep your hands out of your pockets. Avoid having change or keys in your pocket; otherwise, you might be tempted to rattle them as you talk.
- Shirt stays—sort of reverse garters for shirt tails—are a must for men. They not only keep your shirt tucked in but help your posture as well.
- Unless the organizers require it, avoid ties, which generally look old-fashioned in any but the most formal or staid events. If you must wear a tie, stick with solid colors or stripes and avoid cheesy

patterns unless you have a good reason for it. Use a tie clip to keep it in place during your talk. Bring a spare tie in case of spills (or eat spill-resistant foods). And do not wear a tie with a short-sleeve shirt under any circumstances.
- Racerback bras eliminate the issue of slipping straps.
- Don't show off your physique unless it is a key part of your message—for example, if you're speaking about the importance of a regular exercise regimen and want to wear tasteful exercise clothing.
- We can't think of any circumstance where sheer clothing would be appropriate.
- It's always a good idea to pack a shoe cleaning kit.
- Makeup will mask skin imperfections and almost always makes you look better on camera if the talk is recorded. There's a saying in the video industry that "makeup makes money," and it's absolutely true, even for men. Michael has a shiny forehead and sometimes wears makeup on his YouTube channel and at some speaking engagements. However, he got good training from his wife; you shouldn't wear makeup unless you know what you're doing or someone at the event can help you.

Speaker's Notes

Capture your responses to the questions below in the downloadable document available at https://www.theindyauthor.com/from-page-to-platform.html.

- Considering the type of event and venue at which you normally present or to which you plan to pitch yourself, what will your "uniform" outfit be?

BEFORE THE EVENT

In the following sections, we'll review the key actions you need to take before, during, and after your speaker events to discharge your responsibilities as a pro.

Block Your Calendar

Provisionally block your calendar when you pitch an event, because there's nothing more awkward than getting booked for an engagement and then having to decline it because a conflict arose on your end. Blocking your calendar means also confirming your ability to take personal time off from a day job if needed.

Heed Communications from Organizers

You will receive a steady stream of emails from the organizer leading up to the event: news, updates, travel arrangements, venue information, and requests for materials such as slides and information such as food choices for catered meals.

Professionalism as a speaker means always responding

promptly to the organizer's emails. Don't be the speaker who never returns emails. Also, don't pester the organizer or ask them questions that they already provided. Triple check all the information the organizer has sent before you even think about asking a question. It's okay to ask clarifying questions but don't irritate them by demonstrating that you can't be bothered to read their emails.

Manage Your Materials

Provide Material to the Organizer

If your talk includes a presentation (e.g., PowerPoint or similar), be sure to send it to the organizer if, when, and how they request it. Complying with the organizer's guidelines is a key component of professionalism as a speaker.

Send your presentation to the organizer by the deadline—and well before the deadline, if possible. If your slide deck is too large to send via email, upload it to a cloud sharing website and send a link to the organizer so they can download it from there.

Understand what the organizer's plans are for the presentation file. If the organizer asks for a copy of your presentation only so they have a better idea of what you will cover to promote it more effectively, then a nearly final version might be fine, and you can continue to refine it after you've sent the copy.

However, if they plan to upload it to a laptop at the venue and have it ready for you when you arrive, you need to send them the final version—and only once. Double- and triple-check every slide before hitting *Send*. Sending multiple iterations causes the organizer headaches and makes you look disorganized. It also increases the risk that the wrong version gets loaded for your actual talk. (That said, if you discover a critical error with your slides, such as missing content or incorrect or outdated information, that is a good reason to send an updated version. Be sure to name the file so that it's clear that it's a new version—e.g., appending v2 to the file name—and confirm with the organizer that they have received the revision.)

In our experience, organizers rarely provide input on slide contents—it's more common for them to revise your talk's title to make it more marketable to the venue's audience—but you should be prepared for such feedback. If they ask you to add, edit, or delete something, oblige, and provide a revision quickly. Don't fight them about this. They know the event and its audience better than you do, and their feedback will help you increase your chances of a successful talk.

Confirm Your Ability to Share Your Material

Confirm with the organizer whether you can share presentation material outside the event. If they allow it, you might use slide excerpts to help promote the event and post the presentation itself on your website for attendees and others to reference. However, not all organizers—especially those running events with paying attendees—will want you to share your presentation. Some organizers will allow you to share it, but only within certain timeframes.

A good rule of thumb, depending on the organizer's agreement, is to post the presentation on your website for attendees of the event, but not to market it to the general public unless the organizer does.

Research Your Fellow Presenters and Event Attendees

Most organizers publicize the speakers who will be giving talks at an event, and many also share information about attendees. Checking these rosters and doing a little online research into the event's other presenters and attendees will not only set you up to provide a compelling talk but can also identify opportunities for networking and community-building.

Promote the Event as well as the Talk

Promote the *event*, not just your talk, to your followers via email newsletter, social media, and elsewhere. Don't forget to tag the organizer in your posts, and find out if the organizer has designated a hashtag for the event and use it when posting on social media. The organizer's goal is to grow their audience, and they rely on their network of speakers as one of the ways they do that.

Check to see if the organizer provides speakers with affiliate links for promoting the event and take advantage of that whenever possible.

Triple Check Your Website

Since the purpose of your talk is to promote your books or other products or services, make sure your website is in good working order, paying special attention to your homepage, pages specific to the offerings you'll be promoting, pages where your books are for sale (check online retail sites as well), and your contact page.

- Confirm that your bio is up to date. If you're preparing for an in-person event, print out a copy to bring with you in case you need to provide it to an organizer who might be introducing you at the start of your talk.

- Check that your Events page is up to date. If it shows an event that took place last year as "upcoming," you'll look unprofessional to your website visitors.
- Triple check links. You don't want to frustrate a potential new follower with an electronic dead end.
- Check that downloadable material is in fact downloadable. Check using different browsers and devices. You may discover that mobile users have trouble downloading your material as you intended. Test the download on both your desktop and your phone to identify potential problems.
- Send yourself a test message from your Contact page to make sure that it gets through. You don't want to solicit people to contact you and then not keep your end of the bargain.

Use the Event App

Some venues provide an app that serves as a virtual "watering hole" for participants. The app will contain everything a participant needs to know about attending the event, such as a session list, event locations, and even chat rooms for participants to connect. The event app is a great way to meet people, set up meal buddies, and ask questions of other participants. You may also receive questions from participants about your session via the app.

If You Have to Cancel

There may be times when, despite your best efforts, you have to cancel. Michael once had to have emergency surgery, which required him to cancel a paid speaking engagement 48 hours before the event.

Determining when to cancel is a delicate balance. You want to cancel early enough that the organizer has time to make alternate arrangements, but you don't want to make the decision so early that you find you have cancelled an engagement you could have discharged. You also don't want to aggravate the organizers by vacillating between "I think I can" and "I think I can't." Only you and the organizer can judge what the right balance is for each circumstance, but in our opinion, it's better to cancel early than late, even if it means losing the opportunity; the organizer will appreciate sufficient notice. In fact, you might be able to help the organizer out (and pay it forward to a fellow speaker) if you have in mind a possible replacement speaker. However, if you do this, check with the replacement speaker first to make sure they're available and open to the request.

For In-person Events

Confirm Your Travel

Confirm your travel and hotel reservation, ideally via phone. This is a good practice if you've booked the travel yourself, but it's doubly important if the organizers have booked your travel for you. Hotels and airlines often have apps that can make tracking travel easier. These apps also provide additional useful information, such as airline baggage and carry-on requirements.

Pre-arrange Meetings with Fellow Presenters and Event Attendees

One of the many ways speaking engagements can support your author career is by providing opportunities to build community with your colleagues and with fans and followers, current and future. In-person events especially provide a great opportunity to do this. Once you've browsed the attendee list and researched those who pique your interest, reach out to anyone with whom you'd like to make a connection. This might be a colleague with whom you've only interacted virtually, or an author in your genre with whom you'd like to propose some cross-promotion activities. (Scheduling get-togethers for meals or coffee has the added benefit of alleviating a possible source of anxiety: having to eat alone.)

If you're an introvert, scheduling these meetings might feel awkward, but most attendees are also looking for community-building opportunities, and if your approach is polite and not pushy, most will be happy for the offer.

Confirm the Venue Tech and Pack Your Own

The list in this section will equip you well for most events but get as much information about the AV setup of the event and venue as you can from the organizers in advance, since it may impact what you need to bring.

Laptop

If you have a laptop, bring it even if the organizers tell you they will provide one. It's cheap insurance in case something goes wrong with the venue's equipment. (It also enables you to make some headway on your work-in-progress, should the opportunity arise.)

Bringing your laptop also means that you need to consider the security of your data. Use a strong password and lock your computer whenever you're not using it. Store it in your hotel room safe.

Electronic and Actual Copies of your Presentation

Bringing a USB drive with a copy of your presentation is inexpensive insurance that your presentation will be available when you need it, especially if you don't bring a laptop. Also save your presentation to the cloud so that you can access it that way if needed. Matty posts a downloadable copy of the presentation on a hidden page on her website, the URL of which she can easily share with a venue's AV staff if they need to download the presentation to a venue computer. And consider bringing a print-out of your slides for your own reference in the worst-case scenario of an electronic version being completely inaccessible.

Speaker's Bag

There are certain tech items you need frequently as a speaker; if you create a speaker's bag with these items, you don't need to worry about reassembling this equipment for each engagement. Below are some ideas for what to include based on our own speaker's bags.

- A **presentation remote** allows you to advance or reverse your slides, revert to a blank screen, and use a laser pointer. Most presentation remotes are USB devices that plug and play with any computer. Remotes are great because you don't have to worry about using a mouse or the arrow buttons on a laptop keyboard. A remote allows you to move freely around the stage, and using your own means you can practice with it and feel comfortable with its operation.
- A **portable USB thumb drive with your slide deck on it** provides coverage in case the venue doesn't load it onto the presentation

computer, or you have to make last-minute changes.
- **Adapters and cables** enable you to hook your computer up to various devices like projectors. You should have an adapter that will connect the port on your computer with an HDMI (High-Definition Multimedia Interface) device. Check your laptop's system information or online sources to confirm its port type. Adapters are especially important for Mac users, since most venues use Windows computers and are equipped to support Windows connections.
- A **charging port / power bank** with cables for your phone, laptop, and any other devices you carry with you is a better option than airport USB outlets, which can be manipulated to steal your data through a method called "juice jacking." Having your own charging port enables you to plug directly into wall outlets at the airport. It also lets you provide your own power whenever you need it.

Start small but try to anticipate anything that you might need. Over time, you'll get a feel for what needs to be in your speaker's bag; experience is the best teacher.

For Virtual Events

Virtual events make conferences more affordable, more accessible to people all over the world, and more convenient. After all, who can beat learning top-notch information in your pajamas on your couch? Even in-person events often have virtual options because it's a lucrative revenue stream for the organizers. This means that speakers will be in more demand than ever before. It also means that giving a great virtual presentation is a required skill for professional speakers.

Resist the urge to spend less time and effort preparing for a virtual presentation just because it's virtual. You should take the same care in preparing for virtual events as for in-person events.

Creating a Virtual Presentation Space

The first step in preparing to speak at virtual events is to create a professional presentation space.

We've all seen speakers give talks in virtual environments that are unprofessional or even cringe-worthy: family members or pets wandering in and out of frame, perhaps seen through an open door in the background; a messy environment, with stacks of papers teetering on desks or clothes thrown untidily over a chair; or the use of a usually private environment like a bedroom for a public event. Our least favorite: presenters who speak while driving a car. These are distractions. If attendees are scanning your background or are worried that you're engaged in a dangerous activity, they're not paying attention to your message.

Distractions can be auditory as well as visual: people speaking in the background, dogs barking, cars honking, and (the bane of Matty's existence) leaf blowers roaring.

If your audience's first exposure to you is in an unprofessional space, you will have a hard time convincing them that you and your talk are worthy of their time and attention. In this section we share tips to ensure that your virtual presentation space is as professionally presented as the content of your talk.

The Space

Almost any room in your home can be made appropriate

as a professional background—except for the bathroom, which offers obvious visual as well as acoustic challenges.

First, consider how protected the space is from visual and auditory distractions. Matty's usual workspace is in her den, which is prone to distractions from activity in the neighboring kitchen and from her dogs. For this reason, she has set up a separate space in a small bedroom that she uses for recording episodes of The Indy Author Podcast as well as for any virtual events she participates in. Because the room contains dressers, which seem more appropriate to a private than a public space, she uses seagrass room dividers to screen them off from camera view. Room dividers, especially if made with a soft material like seagrass or fabric, are also useful for sound absorption, which will improve audio quality as well.

Michael's virtual presentation space is in his basement. The cinder block walls were originally white, which didn't look good on camera, so he painted them purple, suggesting creativity. He also chose padded furniture to help absorb sound for better audio quality.

Consider what the space says about the topic of your talk. If you're discussing a topic of interest to writers, then your writing desk might be a good space. If you're discussing a topic of interest to readers, then a bookcase might be a good backdrop. (Just be sure to vet the titles that your audience will see and consider what message they will send.) If you're talking about how to host a podcast, then the space where you record your podcast would be appropriate.

But what about virtual or blurred backgrounds, you might ask. We're not fans. Unless you're using a high-performance computer and a green screen background, these often result in an indistinct differentiation between the presenter and their background and a distracting ghosting effect (e.g., a presenter's hand appearing when they reach toward the camera and disappearing when they draw it back). But aside from technical concerns, a virtual or blurred background puts up a barrier between you and your audience. Let the people with whom you're interacting see where you're sitting and let them get to know you—the best version of you—through that exposure.

An exception to this general advice against using virtual backgrounds might be for book events, where a virtual background of the book cover seems appropriate and festive. However, don't use such a background as your default, because it's not going to be appropriate for all events, and could be seen as grandstanding if you are a participant in an event focused on someone else.

The Lighting

Once you've selected the space for your presentation, the next step is to optimize it with pleasing lighting. The right lighting can improve the appearance not only of your room but of you as well.

Sunlight is usually the most appealing light. Make sure that you have a way of managing any sunlight coming into the room by using curtains, shades, or room dividers. You don't want to be sweltering in a sunbeam on a hot day. Additionally, too much light—even natural light—will make you look washed out.

Even if your virtual presentation space normally has plenty of sunlight, make sure you're equipped to supplement it with other lights. This could be a light specifically designed for virtual presentations, or just a spare table light from your storage room. (It's a good idea to experiment with what you have around your house before investing in expensive lighting equipment.) Add or remove a light. Adjust them to varying distances from your face or to different heights. Experiment with removing the lampshade. Use light stands to easily adjust the position and height of your lights.

Because the built-in lighting in Michael's basement virtual presentation space is harsh, he uses a professional three-point lighting setup for a softer and more forgiving illumination. The setup includes a light on Michael, a side light for his hair, and a light against his background.

Presentation-specific lighting will have features that normal household lights will not. For example, the light that Matty uses for virtual events has options for warmer (redder) or cooler (bluer) color temperatures. If you're using lights with adjustable color temperature or intensity, don't set it and forget it—adjust them to accommodate the current circumstances. For example, during the day, you may need to turn the intensity up to achieve a noticeable effect, while in the evening, a lower intensity setting will be sufficient.

After every adjustment, give your camera few seconds to adjust to the new lighting situation. Find the set-up that ensures your features are clearly visible but doesn't result in a harsh glare on your skin—too much and too little light are equally distracting. If your audience isn't thinking about your lighting, you've probably done it right.

The Props

Once you've chosen a distraction-free (or at least distraction-resistant) space and lit it in an appealing manner, consider how you can use props to create the impression you want to convey to your audience. Think of how you can brand your space appropriately to your persona. Ask yourself, "Will someone seeing this space want to know more about me? Will they be attracted to or put off by the persona it portrays?"

Matty's virtual presentation space features a poster of a boat under sail, playing on her love of nautical metaphors for the writing craft and the publishing voyage. It also includes an ironwood statue of an owl, which she added for the launch of her novel *The Falcon and the Owl,* and which has been in the background ever since.

Michael's props have changed over the years, but he has a bookcase with fairy lights and glass bottles along with a face-out copy of one of his physical books. They add nice, lowkey ambiance.

As an author, you're a storyteller. Consider the story your props are telling.

The Tech

At an in-person event, you must worry about the first impression. How you act, what you wear, and even how you stand will send subconscious signals to the audience.

First impressions exist virtually too, and the biggest factors that influence them are the professionalism of your audio and video setup. The right camera and microphone will provide a pleasing and professional experience for your audience, better enabling them to absorb your message. The wrong equipment will make them tune out—and maybe even log out.

Because equipment becomes obsolete quickly, we don't provide specific equipment recommendations in this book. Instead, we will offer some best practices and tips to help you find the right equipment no matter when you are reading this book.

While you will have to spend some money on equipment (if you don't have it already), consider this an investment in your author brand that will pay for itself. Good equipment is the cost of entry into the virtual speaking market, and advances in technology are making that equipment both better and less expensive.

Choosing a Camera

We recommend that you follow these best practices when selecting a camera:

- Don't use the built-in webcam on your computer. These webcams are low-quality, are not optimized for low light, and will almost always result in an unflattering look. They are fine for communicating with friends and family, or for having informal conversations, but they are not professional enough for speaking engagements, especially paid ones.
- Look for high-resolution webcams. While it is possible to use a digital single lens reflex (DSLR) camera as a webcam, that is too much firepower for most presenters. You can upgrade your camera later if needed.
- Do a web search for *best webcams <insert current year>*. This will return a list of results with the highest-rated cameras.
- Watch video reviews for webcams to see accurate representations of how you and your background will look.
- We recommend a webcam capable of 1080p resolution. You can certainly purchase a higher resolution webcam, but it is not required.

Cameras aren't cheap, but consider that, not too long ago, high-quality broadcast cameras cost six figures. Now you can find a high-definition camera for whatever your budget may allow. If the price tag seems steep, keep in mind that webcams have high reliability ratings and are likely to last a long time.

Choosing a Microphone

Don't use the built-in microphone on your device. Almost

any auxiliary mic, even a inexpensive one, will provide better sound quality. There are microphone options to suit every budget. Research recommendations for entry-level podcasting mics. Michael paid $120 for his first podcasting microphone, he used it for a decade before upgrading, and its sound quality rivaled that of much more expensive microphones.

Most entry-level podcasting microphones are USB-powered, which means you can plug them into a USB port on your computer. We recommend a USB-powered microphone to keep things simple, at least at the start of your speaker career. The internet is awash with audio snobs who look down on USB-powered podcasting microphones, but the quality is more than sufficient for virtual presentations.

We also recommend the following mic accessories:

- A **pop filter** goes in front of or on the microphone to minimize plosives, a burst of air that comes from your mouth when you pronounce certain consonants such as B and P. Plosives are especially unpleasant for audience members who are listening to your talk through headphones.
- A **shock mount** stabilizes the microphone to prevent desk bumps, shakes, or other vibrations from causing undesired noise in the audio. While not required, you would be surprised how often you accidentally bump your desk or even the microphone while speaking.
- A **boom arm** to which you attach your microphone allows ultimate flexibility in positioning of the mic and clears space on your desk.

The Importance of Wired Internet

We recommend using a wired internet connection for your virtual talk, as well as for any pre-event tech rehearsals; a wired connection will give you a more stable experience.

Michael was once a guest on one of the biggest podcasts in the publishing industry. This was an opportunity of a lifetime. As soon as the interview started, his Wi-Fi connection dropped. He had to run to his neighbor's house, get his neighbor's wireless network password, run back to his house, connect to his neighbor's network, and conduct the rest of the interview out of breath. He swore he would never again use wireless internet for any podcast interview or speaking engagement.

However, there was one problem: he didn't have a wired internet port in his basement office. He hired an electrician to install an internet port in his basement. Now he uses a wired connection any time he is speaking.

It doesn't matter how good your internet is; you're leaving things to chance if you use a wireless signal. If your signal drops, what is your contingency plan? (In reality, your contingency plan is probably to use your phone, assuming you have a cell signal, but that will greatly degrade the experience for you and your audience because the audio quality will be bad, and you won't be able to screenshare.)

If you don't have high-speed internet, let others in your house know you will need extra bandwidth for your event. Ideally, you should be the only one in the house using the wireless network during your event.

Getting Comfortable with Virtual Meeting Platforms

Organizers use many virtual meeting platforms (e.g., Zoom, Microsoft Teams, WebEx) to host their events, and new apps are coming on the market all the time. This section is not a how-to for any specific virtual meeting platform;

rather, it is an overview of best practices that will work well with any platform you may encounter in your speaking career. Fortunately, virtual meeting platforms are more alike than they are different, so if you encounter one you haven't used before, the learning curve should be shallow.

Giving the Platform a Test Run

As soon as you find out which virtual meeting platform an event is using, download it and test it on your computer. Even if you are familiar with the platform, you should still do a quick test to make sure everything is as you remembered. Platforms change their user interfaces often.

If you already have the platform installed on your computer, make sure you update it at least a week before the event. Operating with the latest version will lessen the chances of technical glitches, and making the update well in advance of the event will ensure you have time to test it thoroughly.

If you follow all these steps and on the day of the event still encounter a pop-up that informs you that an update is available, install it only if it's required to launch the platform, or if you run into technical issues. Sometimes new versions introduce new issues, and you don't want to be dealing with those in the hours or minutes leading up to your talk.

If the platform is also available as a mobile application, install and test it on your phone. That way, if the desktop platform is unavailable for any reason, you have the mobile app as back-up.

The Importance of Tech Rehearsals

Many venues will host a tech rehearsal in advance of the event. Always attend the tech rehearsal, even if you are familiar with the platform. The organizer may use an element of that platform that you've never seen before. You may gain valuable logistical information, such as how you will be introduced. Michael once attended a speaking engagement where there was no emcee and no speaker introduction; instead, at the date and time of the event, the organizer would send him a text message telling him to unmute his microphone and camera and begin his presentation. If Michael hadn't been aware of that plan by attending the tech rehearsal, his talk would have gotten off to a rocky start.

Tech rehearsals are generally not long events, and the time you spend to attend them will pay you back in quality of presentation and peace of mind. In addition, the tech rehearsal is a great opportunity to get some face time with the organizer.

Best Practices for Virtual Meeting Platforms

Here are some best practices for getting the most out of whichever platform you will use:

- Use headphones or non-mic'ed earbuds to avoid your mic picking up other participants' audio, which will cause feedback.
- Make sure that the platform recognizes your external webcam and microphone. Some old equipment may not work with the newest platforms.
- Test your microphone. Platforms allow you to record a small sample of you speaking and then play it back for you. If there is a microphone issue, you will know immediately.
- Make sure you know how to access and operate the key functions of the platform: muting and unmuting your mic, turning your camera on and off, screen sharing, and group or host-and-presenter-only chat.

- If you're using multiple screens, be sure you understand what screen will display for participants when you share your screen, and how to switch between screens if needed.
- Some platforms will embed your slides into the platform itself, meaning that instead of using your preferred presentation software, you'll use built-in controls on the platform itself to control your slides. Make sure you know how that functionality works.
- If possible, hop on a test call with a friend or family member and determine how everything looks and sounds.
- Some platforms are private until the day of the event, and you won't be able to use them outside of the tech rehearsal, so make sure you attend that rehearsal because it may be your only chance to test your setup.

The Professional Virtual Presenter

Once you have optimized your virtual presentation space, there is another key element of a successful virtual presentation: you. In fact, if you find yourself having to give your talk from a space you can't easily modify, like a hotel room, your own presence will be even more important to the professionalism of the image you project.

Position the camera at eye level to create a conversational feeling. You can purchase a desk tripod that will enable you to adjust the webcam height.

Position the camera so that the top of the frame is just above your head. Your head, shoulders, and perhaps upper torso should be in the frame, but there shouldn't be much empty space above your head. Don't center your face—

otherwise all that space above your head is wasted, and no one really wants to be looking at your ceiling during your talk.

Once you know that your audience's attention will be directed where you want it to be—on your face—where do you direct *your* attention?

Spend most of the time looking into the camera. Think of the camera as the stand-in for your audience and use this virtual eye contact to engage the audience members more fully in your talk.

If the participants have their cameras on, periodically scan their images because, just as with a live audience, you can glean hints about how your talk is going. Is their attention wandering? Maybe it's time for you to ask them a question. Do they look confused? Check in with them for understanding.

You also want to *occasionally* check your own image. A posture that feels attentive may look belligerent onscreen. An expression intended to look serious might come across as angry. You may be swinging back and forth in your chair without even realizing it, or you may have shifted out of the desired framing. Check in on your video feed occasionally but avoid the temptation to keep your attention there. You want to be talking to your audience, not to yourself, and you miss opportunities to optimize your talk for your audience if you're focusing your attention on yourself and not on them.

Holding the Virtual Event Gremlins at Bay

Here are some final tips to ensure that you've eliminated any of the gremlins that might otherwise impact your virtual presentation.

- Make sure your cell phone is fully charged before the event starts.

- Restart your computer several hours before your event. A restart can eliminate issues such as an application running in the background, which could degrade your computer's performance. Doing it several hours in advance avoids the possibility that your computer will decide to install an update that's still chugging away when your event starts.
- If you lose your internet connection and the platform supports a call-in option, call in and continue the presentation without the slides until your internet is restored. If your presentation is overly reliant on visuals, this will be problematic, so develop a plan about what you would do if this happened, such as posting the presentation on your website (with the organizers' permission) and directing attendees there to download it.
- Make sure you have the organizer's phone number so that you can call or text them in the event of a disaster. The worst time to be looking for the organizer's phone number is when you don't have an internet connection ... and you need an internet connection to get their phone number.
- If you discover that there is a high probability of severe weather during your talk, let the organizer know. You don't want them to overreact, but you do want to give them a heads-up so you can brainstorm a back-up plan. Based on your past experience, let them know whether such outages generally last only a few seconds or usually stretch to hours.
- Consider asking a nearby (*very* nearby) neighbor if

you can use their internet connection if something goes wrong with yours.

You can't plan for everything, but you *can* plan. The organizer will appreciate it, and you will win bonus points with the audience if you are quick on your feet.

Speaker's Notes

Capture your responses to the questions below in the downloadable document available at https://www.theindyauthor.com/from-page-to-platform.html.

- Where will your virtual speaking space be?
- What qualities about your personality do you want your background to convey?
- What props might you include in your background that will accurately reflect your persona and topic and that will support the message you want to convey?
- What steps can you take to ensure that you look your best on camera?
- What are three event-related issues that might arise, and what is your contingency plan for how to address each of them?

ATTENDING THE EVENT

This section on attending the event focuses mainly on in-person events, but we recommend reviewing this information even if you're planning for a virtual event, since many of the concepts have virtual equivalents.

You're Always on Stage

As you know, professionalism is everything, and you should consider yourself to be "on stage" from the moment you leave your house to go to the airport. Treat anyone you encounter while traveling as if they could be a participant at the event—you never know. (Honestly, you should be professional in every interaction you have in your life, regardless of whether you're on stage, but the point bears repeating.)

Be courteous. This applies even if airline, train, or hotel staff tests your patience. Everyone gets frustrated when traveling, and there's a time and place to escalate, but you can still be professional and respectful when you do.

Dress the part of the professional, usually business casual;

you'll receive better treatment from the travel professionals and hospitality staff you encounter. Michael has received airplane seat and hotel room upgrades for this very reason. It's even cooler when the venue pays for your travel, and you receive upgrades on top of that!

Don't be one of those speakers who put on their best impression of being a good person when they're on stage but turn into a monster the moment they step off. Courteous behavior is one of the keys to professionalism, and discourteous behavior undermines any goals of creating connections or nurturing fans for your work. Remember, you're always "onstage," even when you're not onstage.

Scope Out the Venue

Try to arrive at the venue before the conference begins. Take some time to wander around the property and get to know it. Sign in to the Wi-Fi. Find the registration desk, restrooms, and any other facilities you might want to use such as hotel restaurants, fitness centers, and so on.

If possible, scout the room where your presentation will be held. If there's a stage or a platform, walk on it and determine the best places to stand. If you'll be using your own laptop, make sure you'll have access to a power outlet; you don't want to be partway through your carefully crafted presentation and have your battery go dead.

Investigate if and how you might accommodate any special requirements. Matty prefers to have a lectern to hold her notes, even if she's not going to be standing behind it. If the room isn't equipped with a lectern, she asks the organizers if it's possible to add one.

Get a sense of the energy and how the space feels. You

can learn a lot about a room by standing in it for a few minutes. Michael once spoke in a small hotel conference room without an audiovisual system. Because there was no microphone, he had to figure out how loudly he needed to speak for participants in the back of the room to hear him. Fortunately, he was with another speaker the night before, and he was able to test out and adjust his speaking volume accordingly.

At another venue, scouting the room the night before helped Michael avert disaster. He found that the screens were poor quality, and participants would have a difficult time reading the black text on a white background Michael had used for his slides. Furthermore, the room's setup was awkward. There was no lectern for the laptop—Michael was to control the slide advances with a remote—and although there were screens on both sides of the stage, there were no screens for him to see where he was in the presentation without periodically turning his back to the audience. This was especially problematic because his slide deck contained many animation transitions with which he needed to synchronize his speech. He was going to have to give his presentation "blind."

You can bet that Michael raced back to his hotel room and reformatted his slides accordingly. He changed the slide deck background to a dark color and scrubbed all the animations. He also condensed the number of slides so he could remember them better.

Organizers won't always give you all the information you need to optimize your performance in the specific venue; checking the space out in advance of your talk will give you time to regroup as needed.

Audiovisual Setup

The AV Team

Many venues hire audiovisual teams who are responsible for ensuring that the speaker has a microphone and laptop computer loaded with their slides. We recommend connecting with the members of the AV team—ideally the ones who will be assigned to support your talk—as early as possible and aim to make their lives as easy as possible. The relationship you have with the AV team can make (or break) a presentation.

Michael once attended an event where the AV team traveled all over the world to do AV for different events. Once he got them talking over beers, they told him crazy stories about their travels in different countries. The next morning, when it was time for Michael to give his event, you can bet the AV team took extra care of him because he bonded with them in the bar!

Microphones

Try to arrange with the AV team to test the microphone as early as possible (in addition to doing a final test immediately before your talk). Having a basic understanding of mic options will help you work smoothly with the AV team and can enable you to serve as your own AV team, if necessary.

There are three types of microphones:

- handheld
- tabletop
- lapel / lavalier

Handheld microphones have several disadvantages for use during a talk. If you're nervous or your hands are naturally unsteady, participants will notice your hands trembling on the microphone. You lose the ability to use one of your hands. If you don't hold the microphone consistently in the "sweet spot" a few inches from your mouth, your volume will be inconsistent. These microphones tend to go haywire easily; if you accidentally tap the top of the mic, you could create unpleasant feedback. Handheld mics are fine for a standup comedy routine or karaoke performance; other options are better for a professional talk. If the AV team plans to use a handheld mic, ask if there is an alternative.

Tabletop microphones rest on a stand on the lectern (or, with panels, the table). The stands are often flexible so you can angle the mic toward your mouth. Tabletop mics have their own set of challenges. They will tie you to the lectern, eliminating the possibility of creating some energy by moving around the stage. You may have to reposition them frequently. They are often more basic than other types of mics, meaning that the audio quality is not as good. If your computer is on the lectern, moving your head to look at the slides on the monitor will move your mouth out of the microphone's sweet spot. As with handheld mics, ask your AV team if there's an alternative.

Lapel / lavalier microphones are the best option. The microphones themselves clip onto your clothing at lapel level, and a battery pack that powers the mic clips on out of sight, often at the back of a belt or waistband. (This is why we recommend that your speaker "uniform" factor in the need to accommodate a clip-on mic and battery pack.) The greatest benefit of lapel microphones is that once you're mic'ed up, you don't have to worry about them. They're also less prone to technical issues. Audiovisual teams prefer them for this reason too.

One cautionary note about lapel mics: because you wear them, it's easy to forget they're there, and Matty and Michael have both heard speakers engage in what they thought were private conversations when in fact their mic was "hot." Be sure to find out from your AV team how to turn the mic on and off ... and out of an abundance of caution, use the restroom *before* the AV team mics you up.

Laptop / Computer

Audiovisual teams are also responsible for projectors and, where the venue provides them, laptops, but you'll need to ensure that your presentation file is on the laptop and that the correct version is loaded. As a back-up, bring an external hard drive with a copy of your slides, or save your slides to the cloud and make sure you can access them from the venue's computer.

You also need to check that each slide looks the way it should. If the venue-provided computer uses a different operating system than the one you designed your slides on—for example, you design your presentation on a Mac, but the venue provides a Windows computer—or doesn't have the same fonts loaded, your slides might not look the same. It's best if you can catch this in advance so that you can adjust any elements that don't translate well. If possible, ask a friend with the same computer and operating system as the venue will be using to test your slides. Another good back-up is to have a PDF version of your slides, which will look the same on any computer.

The AV team may also provide a remote control for your slides. If the venue provides a remote, test every button to get comfortable with how it works. If you bring your own remote, make sure it works with the venue's computer.

Lighting

Lighting is an item to check out near the time of your talk since venues sometimes provide additional lighting on the day of the event. At one event, Michael's talk was scheduled for a dark hotel conference room with terrible fluorescent lighting. However, on the day of the event, the venue installed high-powered studio rack lights that were like artificial suns. They were so bright that he couldn't look directly into them. They were also so bright that he couldn't see the faces of the participants. When it was time for Q&A, he was careful to stand in a spot on the stage where he could see people's faces clearly.

Be an Active Participant

Once you've confirmed the audiovisual setup of the presentation space, it's time to make the most the event! Even if you haven't identified community-building as a top priority for your speaker career, you greatly diminish the value of in-person events if you don't take advantage of the opportunity to interact with the organizers, your fellow speakers, and the attendees.

As you meet people at the event, ask for their business card and, either on the card or in your contacts app, capture additional information about them: their appearance (so you can more easily recognize them at other events), topics you discussed, any mentions they made of their personal life, favorite sports teams, and so on. Summarize your conversation in enough detail that you can remember it later.

Also capture any follow-ups from your conversation in whatever tool you use for task management—app, email reminder, or sticky note.

The best time to do this work is the day you meet your contacts! The longer you wait, the more you will forget. Your memory will never be as fresh as it is on the date of your connection. Some people like to do this work while traveling home, such as on a plane or train, but we prefer to use that time to relax. Michael's goal is to always have his notes about his contacts complete and their business cards scanned by the time he walks out of his hotel room for the final time. This way, when he returns home, all he has to do is initiate the follow-ups.

We go into more detail about managing and acting on this information when you return home in the section "Capitalizing on Your Connections."

Use Social Media

You can expand your community-building even beyond other event attendees by sharing the experience on social media.

Post photos of yourself at the venue. These might include photos with recognizable features of the venue or location as a backdrop, or a sign or a poster advertising your talk. If the event hosts a banquet or a cocktail party, these are perfect opportunities to grab lots of photos. Before posting, scan everyone who appears in the photo, even if they are in the background, to make sure that you haven't caught someone doing something they wouldn't appreciate being committed to the internet. For the same reason, if you're posting audio, listen to the audio before posting.

Take photos of yourself with attendees and other presenters and share them generously on your social platforms, tagging others in the photo as possible.

Make sure you are aware of any hashtags the organizers have established for the event ... and if they haven't established hashtags, consider suggesting that they do, or implement your own and encourage others to use them!

Let attendees and other presenters know that you're happy to pose for photos with them. They'll know this if they are following your feed, flagged with event hashtags, but feel free to be overt about your willingness.

However, keep in mind that although capturing fodder for social media is useful, it should never be your primary goal. Never let the desire to grab a selfie with an attendee or another presenter pre-empt the opportunity to have a conversation with that person. The first will provide a pleasant blip on your feed. The second may offer an opportunity for you to clarify a point for an attendee about your talk, to form an alliance with a colleague, or to establish a relationship with a mentor.

The exception to this rule? The night before your presentation, forego networking in favor of a good night's sleep.

Manage Your Energy

Many authors are introverts by nature. We sit in a room for hours and make stuff up. That requires an active imagination and a brain that does its best thinking while alone.

If you're an introvert, you'll need to manage your energy while at the event. After all, you're going to be speaking, which means you will be interacting with people far more than might be your natural preference.

Michael and Matty are both introverts, meaning we gain energy being alone and expend energy being with other people. However, when we attend events, we can move into a more extroverted mode. This is because we understand the long-term benefits in terms of community building to be gained from making this effort. Manage and channel your energy at the event, knowing that you'll have time to recover and decompress when you return home.

Although it is hard to relax or to concentrate on anything else during the time leading up to your talk, participate in the other sessions. Your fellow speakers will appreciate your attendance, your fellow attendees will get a chance to know you, and you may gain useful professional experience from those other sessions. Entering into the event fully as a participant can help calm nervousness that might otherwise bubble up if you focused obsessively on your presentation.

Engage in events beyond the presentations. Attending a social gathering will provide a great opportunity for networking and community-building. One of our colleagues recommends "the one-drink rule": commit to spending at least as much time at a social event as it takes to finish one drink (even if that drink is a bottle of water). And remember that you'll never have trouble striking up a conversation with a writer if you are armed with one simple question: "What are you working on?"

That said, don't be afraid to take time in your room or away from the venue to recharge your batteries. When we were both speaking at a conference in New York City, Michael had only been there once previously, so he recharged by sneaking away to see the sights. (If you're never going to be in that location again, you owe it to yourself to do at least one fun thing away from the crowd, either by yourself or with a few other participants.) Matty, on the other hand, is only a quick train ride away from the city, and so when she needed to recharge, she retired to her hotel room.

If you don't do well for extended periods in social situations, be selective about which activities you participate in; don't force yourself to attend every activity the event offers. If you struggle with interpersonal interactions, focus on making a handful of meaningful relationships rather than broad networking. Introverts are often able to manage better in one-on-one situations.

Speaker's Notes

Capture your responses to the questions below in the downloadable document available at https://www.theindyauthor.com/from-page-to-platform.html.

- What are three strategies you will use to manage your energy at an in-person event?
- What is a red flag you'll watch out for that will mean you need to take time to recharge?

THE DAY OF THE PRESENTATION

This section on the day of the presentation focuses mainly on in-person events, but we recommend reviewing this information even if you're planning for a virtual event, since many of the concepts have virtual equivalents.

On the morning of your talk, eat a light but energy-abundant breakfast. Eggs, protein shakes, leafy greens, chia seeds, oatmeal, Greek yogurt, berries, and parfaits will give you lots of energy throughout the day. Items heavy in grease and sugar such as meats and cereals will sap your energy. Drink a glass of water with every cup of coffee or tea you drink, since staying hydrated will make you feel better and will improve your performance.

Calm Your Nerves

Avoid cramming in a final practice run of your presentation; if you've followed our advice, you'll already be properly prepared. You're better off relaxing and enjoying the resources and the information other speakers have to offer.

However, if despite all your preparation you still feel some apprehension about your upcoming talk, you're in good company. Fear of public speaking is perennially cited as one of the most common phobias. (In fact, the admiration you inspire in your audience for overcoming this common fear in order to get up on stage to share your valuable information means you start out your talk with a point already in your favor!)

Block out time in advance of your talk for ten minutes of meditative relaxation. Find a quiet space where you won't be disturbed—your hotel room if you're staying at the venue, perhaps your car if you are not. Close your eyes and clear your mind. Having a calm and clear mind will go a long way toward minimizing your fear.

Feel confident that the careful work you've done in preparation for your talk will stand you in good stead and know that even the most experienced speakers still feel butterflies in their stomach as they prepare to take the stage. Each time you prepare to give a talk, you will feel some apprehension, but channel it into energy you can use to engage your audience. As you progress in your speaker career, the balance will naturally shift from apprehension to energy.

Arrive Early

Arrive at the room early—at least 15 to 20 minutes before your talk begins, or earlier if requested by the organizer. It may not always be possible to arrive in the room so early; for example, many venues have only a few rooms, so someone could be speaking in your room until shortly before your talk is scheduled to start. Be ready to take possession of the room as soon as possible after the previous speaker is done.

Confirm the Logistics

Ideally, this won't be your first visit to the room. If you've arrived at the venue well in advance, you've already had a chance to check it out. Now is the time when you can make final logistical adjustments.

Do a final test of the **microphone and sound system**. Solicit input about the acoustics from someone sitting where the audience will sit and confirm how close to or far from the mic you should be for the best sound quality.

If video of your talk will be recorded, note where the **camera** is so you can ensure you stay within its frame and can guard against blocking its view of the screen.

Have **water** or other event-appropriate beverage available in case your throat gets dry, or in case you need an excuse to take a moment to organize your materials or your thoughts. In an accommodation for her chronically unsteady hands, Matty avoids having ice cubes in her beverage so that they don't rattle when she takes a drink. In fact, it's best to opt for room temperature beverages because cold water will chill your vocal cords, which will affect the timbre of your voice, and hot water can also negatively distort your voice.

Confirm who will **introduce** you. If a member of the event will do that, make sure they have the information they need; be prepared to give them a printed copy of your bio. If the organizers let you pick whether you would rather self-introduce or be introduced, consider the tone you want to set for the event. If it's a more formal event, you may choose to be introduced; if more informal, to introduce yourself. Being introduced might elevate your status in the eyes of the audience; introducing yourself enables you to begin your interaction with the audience immediately.

Also confirm who will be acting as **timekeeper**. In some cases, the organizer might hold up cards indicating the time remaining. (Confirm whether the time includes or excludes the Q&A portion.) Alternatively, the venue may ask you to keep track of time yourself. Although your practice sessions will have given you a sense of the timing of your talk, it's helpful to remind yourself to double-check your progress at certain slides. We recommend bringing a watch, since you can check the time more easily with a watch than on your phone. Consider taking the watch off and putting it on the lectern next to the laptop so that you can surreptitiously glance at it in between slides rather than looking obviously at your wrist.

Don't ask the organizer—or, even worse, the audience—for time checks during your talk. It breaks your concentration and reminds the audience about the upcoming post-talk break. You want to keep them engaged in your talk, not thinking about the clock.

A quick note related to virtual events: Before signing onto the meeting platform, scan the space behind you. Is there an open door that you intended to close? Is there a tangle of electrical cords that can be moved out of frame? Assess the sound environment. Do you need to shut off a humidifier or other loud electrical appliance?

Mingle with the Participants

Another reason to arrive at the room early is so you can greet participants as they enter. If you have a handout, now is a great time to distribute it to people as they walk in the door. Alternatively, you can set out the handouts in a convenient spot (probably near the door, not near the stage) and point people to it. Chatting with the participants before the talk is something that many speakers don't do, but it will relax you and enable you to start building rapport with your audience even before your talk begins.

Capture the Moment

Before your presentation begins, ask someone in the audience to take a picture of you during the talk. This might be a member of the event staff or a friend, but even strangers are usually happy to oblige—it makes them feel more a part of the action. (Even if an organizer is in the room, don't assume they will take photos if you don't ask.) Ask them to capture not only a close-up of you on stage, but also a photo from the back of the room that includes the audience from the back.

If you're using a laptop, another fun photographic memento of your talk is to take a photo of your screen displaying the title slide of your talk, with the audience out of focus in the background. (This addresses the issue of some audience members who might not want their faces to appear in a photo.) Ideally take the photo as close to the beginning of your talk as possible so the room is as full as it will be during your talk.

Speaker's Notes

Capture your responses to the questions below in the downloadable document available at https://www.theindyauthor.com/from-page-to-platform.html.

- Consider whether there is a tactic beyond the ones we mention that you will find calming if you need to settle some pre-talk nerves.

- What are some ways you might interact with audience members as they enter the room in order to build rapport?

GIVING THE BEST TALK OF YOUR LIFE

This section on giving the best talk of your life applies to both in-person and virtual events.

The Main Event

The moment you've been waiting for has arrived! It's time to execute on all the hours of preparation and hard work you've put into your talk.

If the organizer introduces you, you can jump right into your presentation. Otherwise, introduce yourself to the audience, establishing your credibility and why you deserve to be on stage and speaking on your topic. Depending on your read of the audience, you might preface your formal introduction with some more informal conversation—something all the attendees will be able to relate to, ending on something funny or thought-provoking—to build rapport and "warm up the crowd."

For example, before a panel discussion at a crime writer and reader conference, Matty warmed up the crowd by sharing a story of how the saga of an escaped prisoner near her home in Pennsylvania eerily mirrored the plot of one of her suspense novels.

Michael once gave a talk at eight o'clock in the morning to a group of participants who had traveled to the conference from around the world. He joked sympathetically about the challenges of jet lag and "travel hangover," and promised to do his best not to put everyone to sleep. That got a laugh, and it warmed up the group.

In another talk he gave at a hotel venue that didn't provide breakfast, he raised a few quizzical eyebrows by sharing the tip that the gas station next door offered excellent breakfast pizza. The idea amused the participants—and sure enough, several of them wandered over to the gas station at the first break.

Warming up the crowd not only builds rapport, but also serves another purpose: it takes the edge off your nerves. It's amazing how the fear dissipates once you get people laughing.

However, we recommend steering away from actual jokes. You never know what will offend someone. Keep your remarks congenial. The goal is not to be a comedian—it's merely to get the crowd engaged.

If you will be providing a copy of the slide deck after the talk, let the participants know this upfront so that they don't feel they need to focus their energy on transcribing or photographing your slides.

Read the participants' faces. If people look confused, slow down. If they're nodding their heads, then it means they understand what you're saying so you can keep your current pace. In virtual sessions, if you can't see the audience members, you will need to rely on an organizer or moderator to help judge this based on audience members chat comments or questions, or you may need to more explicitly check in with audience members to give you an indication of their understanding.

Heed your progress against your quarter, half, and three-quarters markers, and adjust your delivery tempo accordingly.

Focus on serving your audience, not on monitoring your performance; this will help calm any anxiety you may be feeling, and your audience will sense and appreciate this focus.

Q&A

No matter how thorough your presentation is, your audience will have questions. A healthy number of questions indicates that you've engaged your audience's interest and piqued their curiosity. Therefore, it's important to recognize that your talk doesn't end when you bring up the last slide. In fact, a solid Q&A session can turn a great talk into an outstanding talk. Q&A sessions are also an opportunity to provide clarification on content that participants didn't understand or to dive deeper into topics of special interest to them. They are your final opportunity to reiterate your message.

Here are some best practices for Q&A for both in-person and virtual events:

- During the Q&A, leave up a slide that shows your contact information, the book you're featuring, and any other information that will help the audience members remember and find you later; a slide that says *Thanks* or *Q&A* is wasted real estate that doesn't provide any value to you or the audience.
- Answer questions quickly, comprehensively, and succinctly.

- Keep an eye on the clock. Your goal is to answer as many questions as possible—all of them if you can. The more questions you answer during the session, the less follow-up work you will have to do afterward.
- Use the questions as a barometer for how well people understood your content. If you receive no questions, it either means that you crushed your presentation or that people weren't interested. Which is it? Why? Paying attention to the audience members' faces and body language will immediately answer that question.
- If the question is very specific to the questioner's situation, try to reframe it in a more general way so your answer will have value for all the participants.
- When answering questions, use affirmative language and avoid any language that seems to demean the questioner. Don't say that the questioner's statement is wrong or inaccurate; express what you know to be the correct information. While it's true that there is such a thing as a dumb question, you should always answer every question with care, attention, and a willingness to help.
- Be prepared for people who ramble and never get to their question. The best way to handle this is to wait for an opening and say, "I'm following you, but what is your question?" This will hopefully get them to pick up the pace. Then, answer the question as quickly as possible to make up for the lost time.

- Be prepared for people who just want to use their time to make a statement. Sometimes this can be productive for the conversation; other times, not so much. Acknowledge them and move on.
- If the session isn't recorded, ask an event staff member or audience member volunteer to capture the questions for your later review. The questions the audience asks may indicate opportunities for refinement of your material or delivery.
- Some talks require interaction from the audience while you're giving your presentation. If your topic invites audience participation, you may want to stop a few times to ask for audience feedback. This is a wonderful way to boost engagement for your talk, but you must always be aware of time. Your biggest problem will be corralling the audience, answering questions quickly, and moving on without leaving people behind.

Organizers sometimes specify how much time to allocate to Q&A, but if they don't, here are our suggestions:

- For a 30-minute talk, at least five minutes
- For a 45-minute talk, at least 10 minutes
- For a 60-minute talk, at least 15 minutes
- For a 90-minute talk, at least 20 minutes

In-person Q&A

If you're conducting a Q&A at an in-person session, here are some best practices to keep in mind:

- Understand the logistics of the Q&A, especially regarding the microphone setup. If you're speaking in a small room, the organizer may not provide a microphone for participants to ask their questions, but if you're speaking in a large room, they very likely will. In this second case, there are a few possible scenarios:
- Participants will pass the microphone around – Make sure you give the microphone enough time to circulate.
- Organizers will act as "runners," delivering the microphone to people who have questions – Be prepared to help direct the organizer to the people with the questions.
- There will be a microphone stand where participants can line up to ask their questions – If the line is long, you may need to speed up the pace of your answers to get to everyone or be ready to volunteer to address any unanswered questions after the talk.
- Repeat the questions, even if participants are using a microphone, to make sure everyone hears the question. Simply say, "The question is..." If the question was long-winded, try to restate it more succinctly.
- Once you have restated the question, pay attention to the participant's face. Are they nodding? Are they giving you other clues to indicate that you restated it correctly? If the answer is yes, then proceed with answering the question. If the answer is no, they will usually clarify. Again, this is why restating the question works to everyone's benefit. It's not productive if

you answer a question that the participant didn't ask. If you can't get to the heart of the participant's question, offer to speak with them after the talk to avoid the Q&A session turning into a one-on-one conversation.
- If it's not possible to reframe a question to apply beyond the questioner's specific situation, offer to speak with them one-on-one after the session so as not to disengage the rest of the audience.
- If audience members still have questions when your time is up, let them know you're happy to answer their questions afterwards, if possible; move these conversations out of the presentation room so the organizers can get it set up for the next speaker.

Virtual Q&A

In this section, we'll address how virtual Q&As differ from in-person Q&As, the several forms that a virtual Q&As can take, and how you can best work with a moderator to handle these, or how you can manage them yourself if you're flying solo. It's always useful to have a moderator for virtual events to help manage the technology and the participants' interactions with it, and this benefit is most apparent in the Q&A portion of your talk.

One way that Q&As differ for virtual events is that in an in-person event, it's easier to direct participants to consolidate their questions into a planned Q&A segment of the talk, whereas virtual participants will likely be logging questions as the questions strike them. This means that you or your moderator will need to monitor for questions throughout your talk. However, you shouldn't jump on every question as it appears —this will cause your talk to be choppy and disjointed.

Addressing questions posed in a virtual setting can be more challenging than at in-person events. They may be presented more informally, and therefore less clearly, and you may have to read between the lines to understand them or spend more time trying to get clarification. Another possible challenge is that you may not be able to have a direct interaction with the questioner if you're working with a moderator.

A way in which virtual Q&A can be *easier* than their in-person counterparts, at least if participants are typing in their questions, is that you or your moderator can vet and triage questions, ensuring equitable distribution among the participants and managing "question hogs" that can try to take over in-person Q&As.

Virtual Q&As can follow a couple of different formats.

The format where participants **"come on stage"** is most like an in-person event where participants line up at a mic to ask their questions. In the virtual scenario, the audience member will unmute their microphone and may turn on their camera. Technology is the biggest pitfall. Unless you have a moderator helping you, be prepared to remind people to unmute their microphones, and to explain to them how to do that. Also remind them to re-mute their mic when they are done asking their question.

The format where participants **submit text questions** is the most different from an in-person event. For example, while sidebar conversations during in-person events are the exception to the rule, the virtual equivalent—chats—are often going on during your talk. To exacerbate the complexity, it's sometimes hard to distinguish the actual questions the audience members have from more general comments they may log.

If you have a moderator; confirm that they will monitor the chat and/or Q&A and feed you the questions that you need to answer. Ask them to provide information in the chat, such as links you might reference during your talk. This can avoid having to spend valuable Q&A time answering logistical question like "Can you say again what that link was …?" Moderators are especially valuable for addressing questions related not to the topic of your talk but to the operation of the virtual meeting platform.

Having a moderator is especially helpful for virtual events because otherwise you will not only have to manage your performance but also manage the tech and monitor the remote participants. Your success with this virtual Q&A style will come down to how well you can multitask, connect with the audience, and improvise when things go off-track. It will also depend on how well-designed the platform's Q&A tool is and how familiar you are with it.

For this reason, we recommend that if the organizer doesn't automatically assign a moderator to help manage the virtual Q&A, you ask for one. If they are unable to do this, consider hiring one. While it may require you to pay the moderator (and therefore give up some of your conference fee if the gig is paid), it will ensure a smoother event experience. You can find people to fulfill this role on freelancer websites, and you should hire them not only for the main event but for the tech rehearsal as well. Work with the organizer to ensure that your assistant has the needed access to the virtual platform.

Michael once taught at a large virtual event where the venue used a clunky conference call platform. Everything about it seemed cobbled together, and the worst part about it was that the Q&A feature required a lot more brainpower than it should have. Michael hired an assistant to catalog the questions, mark which ones were answered, and gather all the unanswered questions in a list so that Michael could answer them in an email to the organizer after the talk. This way, Michael could focus on giving the talk without having to worry about the tech.

If for whatever reason you must "fly solo," here are a couple of tips:

- You might sign on early and offer assistance to any other early arrivers who are having technical difficulties with the meeting platform, but under no circumstances allow questions about the platform to derail you from the focus of your talk.
- If the meeting platform offers separate fields for questions (versus more general chat comments), let participants know that you will monitor questions entered into the dedicated Questions field, but not the chat. If the platform doesn't support a dedicated Questions field, then ask the participants to preface their questions with some easily identifiable marker, such as *QUESTION* in all caps.

Wrapping up the Q&A

These tips about wrapping up a Q&A apply to both in-person and virtual events.

Sometimes audiences won't have any questions, and that's okay. Make a final call for questions, give a long pause—a little longer than might feel comfortable—and if there are still no questions, end the talk and thank everyone for their time.

Sometimes the audience members will have more questions than time allows you to address. If this happens, you have a few options:

- If the organizer allows it, stay in the room or on the call until everyone's questions are answered. If in person, you may need to leave the room so that it can be reset for the next speaker.
- As possible, follow up with participants with answers to any questions you can't answer during the event. (For virtual events, save the chat log to your computer before the call ends so you have a record of these.) The organizer can disseminate the answers, or you can include responses on the event page on your site that you sent the audience to.
- Invite audience members to submit their questions to you via email. Promise to respond to all questions within 24 hours, and then do it.
- If you're video or audio savvy, record responses to the unanswered questions in one of those formats and then either send it to the organizer or include a link on your event page.

Remember that the audience has given up time and often money to see your talk. In some cases, they are making significant sacrifices to attend the event you're speaking at. If they have questions, do your utmost to make sure they receive good answers. Your response could be the one thing they needed to justify attending the event. It could even change their lives.

Dealing with Hecklers

In our experience, hecklers are extremely rare, although the more controversial your topic, the more likely you are to have to deal with them. (And if you bring an aggressive or confrontational tone to your talk, you can expect the same from your audience.)

In any case, it's good to think through your response in advance. Although a commercial jet being disabled by a flock of geese is extremely rare, we're all grateful that Captain Sullenberger had considered what steps he would take if the situation were to arise. Apply that same advance planning to your speaker events.

Many events, both virtual and in-person, have zero-tolerance harassment policies and are likely to take any negative interactions with speakers very seriously. Discuss with the organizers ahead of time how they would address such a situation.

To protect yourself emotionally in this uncomfortable situation, try to keep in mind that the hecklers are probably heckling your message, not you personally. In fact, it may not be about you *or* your message—some hecklers try to make it about themselves, and in doing so, they make themselves look bad. You'll win over other audience members if you're gracious but firm in your response. Resist the urge to get into a verbal battle because that's what hecklers want you to do. Be especially cautious with hecklers if your talk is being recorded.

Consider what is prompting the heckler. Although sometimes their goal is just to get a rise out of a speaker, sometimes there is a legitimate question or point embedded in their heckle. Look for these and, if you perceive such a question or topic, address the question and not the tone in which it was delivered.

Even if the heckler has a point, you must manage the interaction carefully.

- Direct your response to a heckler's question (assuming it's answerable) to the whole room, not specifically to the heckler—otherwise you risk making it a two-person debate that will be hard to extract yourself from.
- Don't move closer to them—this, too, makes it a conversation between the two of you rather than an interaction between you and the larger audience.
- Don't heckle back; your job is to set and model the tone you want from the audience members.
- If they're persistent but seem reasonable, tell them that it's a better conversation to have one-on-one, and that you'll speak with them after the talk (and then follow through).

Virtual presentations may pose a higher possibility of hecklers because of the actual or perceived anonymity of the virtual platform. As with in-person events, address legitimate questions based on the content, not the tone. If a participant becomes hostile or harassing, you or the moderator should know how to mute them or even kick them out of the meeting.

For in-person events, ideally you will have an organizer or representative in the room who can intercede. The larger the audience, the more likely you will have an organizer rep, or even venue staff, in the room with you. However, especially in a smaller setting such as a conference breakout room, an organizer may not be present; even if such a person is there, they might not be willing or prepared to step in.

It's uncomfortable to think about the possibility of needing to protect yourself physically, but any scan of the news will show that it is a possibility, albeit an exceedingly unlikely one. If the heckler won't desist and you're not getting any help from the organizers, in the worst case you might have to bring the session to a close. Obviously, this should be a last-ditch option since you're not only inconveniencing the attendees and the event organizers, but also putting any payment due to you at risk.

In the extremely unlikely event that you fear a physical altercation, leave the stage and seek out event venue staff who can assist you.

For more advice on handling hecklers, review the information from The Alliance of Independent Authors at https://selfpublishingadvice.org/author-safety/ or search for *Author Safety: How Indie Authors Can Protect Themselves Online and Off*.

As noted, these scenarios are exceedingly rare, but thinking through your options in advance will make you better prepared to deal with these situations should they arise.

Be the Last to the Leave the Room

After your talk and Q&A session is over, if the venue and speaker schedule allow it, stay around the stage so that participants can approach you to ask questions. If you must leave the room (for example, because it must be made available for another talk), take the conversation into the hallway and answer questions there. Don't leave the area until everyone in the audience has their questions answered.

This is an opportunity for participants who couldn't ask their question during the Q&A session. It's also an opportunity for people who may have had a question but didn't want to share it with the larger group or derail the conversation. Give these participants the time they need.

Michael once attended a presentation in law school where a guest keynote speaker delivered an amazing presentation.

The speaker was an illustrious judge with a distinguished background. He captivated everyone in the audience, and throughout the presentation, everyone was remarking what a fantastic opportunity it was to hear this man speak. He concluded his presentation and received a standing ovation.

Then, when the applause died down, he leaned into the microphone and said, "Thank you everyone. Now if you don't mind, I am going to the stadium to watch the women's basketball game." He walked out of the room, shut the door behind him, and left everyone in the audience staring at each other. Some thought it was a joke. As the silence continued, everyone realized that the speaker had truly left. If he had stayed for even a five-minute Q&A session, he would have left the audience satisfied with their experience, not irritated at his rudeness.

Leaving the room too early will make you look out of touch and as if you don't want to interact with participants. That's a bad signal to send if you want to speak professionally. Being the last to leave sends the opposite signal—that you are there to listen and help.

Speaker's Notes

Capture your responses to the questions below in the downloadable document available at https://www.theindyauthor.com/from-page-to-platform.html.

- Which five of the tips we've shared in this section about giving the best talk of your life will you put on the top of your own reminder list to review in advance of any talk?

AFTER YOUR TALK (IT'S NOT OVER WHEN YOU STEP OFF THE PODIUM)

Recharge and Celebrate!

Congratulations! You have delivered the best talk of your life (just one of many) and have stepped off the actual or virtual podium. You've expanded your circle of fans and followers and may have caught the eye of other event organizers. If you traveled to an in-person event, you have had some learnings yourself and built your community of fellow authors and your network of fellow speakers.

Speaking engagements can be mentally, emotionally, and physically exhausting, and you deserve some much-needed rest. But there are a few things you should do before you move your attention to your next engagement. If you're traveling home by plane or train, you can even follow the steps in this section while you're on your way home. That way, when you get home, you can truly relax.

Tick off the Tasks

Follow up immediately on any pending tasks left over from the event. If you promised your audience that you'd post an update to the presentation on your website, do that right away. If you need to confirm that your hotel charges were correct, don't delay. These tasks will be easier and faster to take care of the sooner you address them. You'll cement your reputation as a speaking professional if you can confirm to attendees, fellow speakers, and organizers that the tasks you promised to perform are not just on your to do list but are done.

Follow up with the Organizers

One of the most important things you can do after the event is thank the organizers. Whether they approached you or whether you approached them, they were kind enough to make you part of their event. That is worthy of a heartfelt thank you.

Send a thank you email to the organizer who invited you as well as to other staff members you worked with directly, such as coordinators, concierges, panel moderators, A/V technicians, and emcees. You might even consider handwritten thank you notes if you have mailing addresses—we can guarantee that that extra effort will make you stand out from the crowd.

This is also the perfect time to ask for a brief testimonial if they are willing to give one. Ask for it as soon as possible after the event while it is fresh in the organizer's mind. To make their lives even easier, provide them with information to jog their memories, such as the title of the talk and a one- or two-sentence summary of the content. If you have any complimentary comments from attendees, you could even quote these as fodder for the testimonial! As tired as *you* are, remember that the organizer is likely to be ten times more so. Make it as easy as possible for them to comply with this request.

If the organizer requires an invoice to pay you, send it now to expedite your payment.

Capitalize on Your Connections

If you have truly been an active participant in the event, you will have met a lot of people. Your supply of your own business cards will have dwindled, replaced by all the business cards you collected. If you follow our advice in the section on "Being an Active Participant" as well as the later section on "Business Cards," then you'll have notes to remind you about the person behind each card.

Immediately after the event, separate the cards into two categories: those you can discard and those that represent a valuable follow-up opportunity.

Many of the cards that go into the discard pile will be ones you received from "flybys." Flybys are the people who hand out business cards indiscriminately, before either of you have any sense of who the other person is, what the connection between the two of you might be, and if there is any value in nurturing such a connection. A card on which you've made no notes is probably from a flyby. You might also have cards from people who don't represent a business opportunity, even if you had an enjoyable conversation with them in the bar. Discard those cards. You don't want to clutter up your contact list with people you have no intention of following up with.

The other pile will represent worthwhile contacts with whom you want to follow up. This might include setting up a meeting, brainstorming ideas for collaboration, asking for an introduction to another worthwhile contact, or continuing the conversation you had about a shared interest. The best follow-ups are done within 24 to 48 hours of the event, while "event buzz" is still in effect; failure to do so might forfeit a valuable opportunity. These contacts are the ones for which a handwritten note is worth the time and effort. It's rarely done these days, but it adds a great personal touch and increases the chances of building a relationship with the person.

Scan the cards of the worthwhile contacts into your phone's contact list and discard the physical card; you don't want to be trying to track down physical cards when you need the person's contact information.

By acting on all your follow-ups promptly, you will maximize your benefits from the event and capitalize on potential opportunities.

Share the Experience

Advertising the conference on your social media channels is a smart thing to do, and often required in your speaker agreement. However, for out-of-town events, we recommend you hold your posts until you are back home. News articles abound of people broadcasting their away-from-home plans, only to return to a ransacked house. Burglars do pay attention to social media channels.

Update Your Website

This is also a great time to update the speaker page on your website to show that you spoke at the event. Get a logo for the event and display it prominently on your speaker page. As allowed by the organizers, include a photo of you speaking at the event or audio or video clips from the talk—even your presentation. By updating your speaking page, you make yourself more marketable to future organizers who happen upon your website. This is a critical step if you want to land more engagements in the future.

Speaker's Notes

Capture your responses to the questions below in the downloadable document available at https://www.theindyauthor.com/from-page-to-platform.html.

- What are three concrete tasks you will commit to doing after every event to capitalize on the opportunities to support your speaker goals (e.g., earning direct or indirect income, building a professional network, etc.)?

YOUR SPEAKER TOOLKIT

Every profession has a toolkit, and professional speakers are no different. In this section, we explore what tools you need to have to pave the way to a successful author speaker career.

Media Kit

Your media kit is the public-facing component of your speaker toolkit—the material you will make available to organizers for all the information they need related to you as a speaker. We discuss this in terms of online resources, but most of these can be translated into physical versions if needed.

Common components of a media kit are:

- Bios – We explore that in the "Speaker Bios" section.
- Photos – We explore that in the "Headshot" section.
- Book cover images and synopses – These provide an opportunity to highlight the book(s) you want to promote as part of your speaker career.

- High level accomplishments and achievements, including awards
- Contact information
- Social media links
- Sample interview questions – These can be not only a valuable service to interviewers but can also benefit you by enabling you to steer conversations toward topics that best meet your speaker goals.

Having a media kit can attract speaking opportunities, since it demonstrates your professionalism. Organizers can assess your material to help them evaluate whether you are a good fit for their event.

Speaker Bios

Your speaker bio is your opportunity to describe your experience, your areas of expertise, and your achievements, which are key to pitching yourself successfully for speaking engagements. Your bio also introduces the audience to you, often many months before the event begins. Along with a strong presentation title, the bio will help participants determine if your talk will be worth their time and possibly money to attend.

Different organizers will want different amounts of biographical data, usually expressed in terms of maximum word count, so it makes sense to create one master bio with all your information and then shorten it as needed to meet an organizer's requirements. In addition, the same organizer will want bios of different lengths for the same event—for example, one to assess your qualifications to speak (the long bio) and one to use to introduce you in advance of your talk (an introduction bio). And you'll also want a one-liner in your mental pocket—for example, to use to introduce yourself at author social events. We describe the components of the different versions below.

Long Bio

The long bio, from which you can extract shorter versions, should include all the information you might want to share with an event organizer or your target audience.

Your long bio should include:

- If needed, a phonetic representation of your name (and any other components of your bio that might be mispronounced); for example *Matty Dalrymple (DAL-rim-ple)*
- A list of your works
- Major speaker events, including talks, podcast appearances, webinars, classes, etc.
- Awards
- Significant achievements
- Contact information
- A bit of personal information to humanize you, like your hobbies, where you live, or fun facts

Consider that organizers may excerpt material from your long bio for promotional purposes, and that any material you send them may be shared on a variety of platforms. Unfortunately, formatting does not always carry forward to other platforms, so you may, for example, lose italics that you've used to format the titles of your books. Unless the effect looks shouty, consider capitalizing as well as italicizing your titles so that even if the formatting drops out, the titles will still be set off from the other text.

Make sure the information you include is curated, not

exhaustive. If you were creating a resumé to apply for an upper-level management position, you wouldn't include your high school job working at the local fast-food franchise. Similarly, a less well-known award you won early in your author career, while perhaps valid fodder for your speaker bio at that time, may appear out-of-place once you start adding other, more well-known awards. Review your bio periodically to ensure that the information you include is portraying you as the speaker professional you are.

Here is an example of Matty's long bio (~300 words):

Matty Dalrymple (DAL-rim-ple) podcasts, writes, speaks, and consults on the writing craft and the publishing voyage as The Indy Author. Since 2016 she has hosted hundreds of episodes of THE INDY AUTHOR PODCAST; she is also the author of THE INDY AUTHOR'S GUIDE TO PODCASTING FOR AUTHORS. Writer's Digest has named TheIndyAuthor.com one of the "101 Best Websites for Writers."

She is the co-author, along with Mark Leslie Lefebvre, of TAKING THE SHORT TACK: CREATING INCOME AND CONNECTING WITH READERS USING SHORT FICTION and, along with Michael La Ronn, of FROM PAGE TO PLATFORM: HOW TO SUCCEED AS AN AUTHOR SPEAKER. Matty's articles have appeared in Writer's Digest magazine.

Matty has appeared as a presenter and podcast guest, speaking about independent publishing, short fiction, story framing, publishing tips for frugal authors, and more in venues including the Writer's Digest Conference, the Alliance of Independent Authors' SelfPubCon, International Thriller Writers CraftFest conference, Joanna Penn's The Creative Penn Podcast, Mark Lefebvre's Stark Reflections on Writing and Publishing Podcast, Sacha Black's The Rebel Author Podcast, Jeff Elkin's The Dialogue Doctor Podcast, the Kobo Writing Life Podcast, Dale Robert's Self-Publishing with Dale YouTube channel, the Women in Publishing Summit, the Bay Area Writers' League, and many more.

Matty serves as the Campaigns Manager for the Alliance of Independent Authors. You can connect with The Indy Author at TheIndyAuthor.com and on Facebook and YouTube.

Matty is also the author of the four-book Lizzy Ballard Thrillers series, beginning with *ROCK PAPER SCISSORS*, which was named a Notable Indie by Shelf Unbound magazine; the six-book Ann Kinnear Suspense Novels series, beginning with *THE SENSE OF DEATH*; and the Ann Kinnear Suspense Shorts, including *CLOSE THESE EYES*.

Matty is a member of International Thriller Writers and Sisters in Crime. You can connect with Matty at MattyDalrymple.com and on Facebook.

Matty lives with her husband, Wade Walton, and their dogs in Chester County, Pennsylvania. She enjoys vacationing on Mount Desert Island, Maine, and Sedona, Arizona, and these locations provide the settings for her work.

Here is an example of Michael's long bio (~200 words):

Michael La Ronn (la-RAHN), also known as M.L. Ronn, has published over 100 science fiction & fantasy novels and self-help books for writers.

His fiction includes the urban fantasy Good Necromancer series, the dark fantasy Last Dragon Lord series, and the futuristic science fiction Android X series. Currently, he writes primarily urban fantasy.

His nonfiction books for writers include the best-selling *BE A WRITING MACHINE*, which teaches how to beat writer's block forever, and *THE POCKET GUIDE TO PANTSING*, which explains how to write a novel without an outline (with confidence).

Michael also runs the award-winning YouTube channel "Author Level Up," with over 40,000 subscribers and 2 million views. Writer's Digest voted the channel one of the "Best Resources for Writers" in 2020.

Michael devoted himself to the writing life in 2012 after a near-death experience, writing 10 to 12 books per year despite working a demanding full-time job as an insurance executive, raising a family, and attending law school classes in the evenings. His productivity methods are so effective that his YouTube subscribers have accused him of being a cyborg in disguise (he pleads the fifth).

For more information on Michael's books, visit his fiction website at michaellaronn.com and his resources for writers at authorlevelup.com.

You can use your long bio not only for your media kit but also on the About page of your website. Just consider tweaks you might want to make depending on the visitors you expect to that site; for example, Matty de-emphasizes the details of her work as The Indy Author in her fiction-centric MattyDalrymple.com website.

Once you have your long bio in place, you can excerpt from it for various needs. We've listed some examples below.

Introduction Bio

The introduction bio is the bio the host will read to attendees before your talk. The goal of the introduction bio is to give the attendees just enough information to remind them of why you are well qualified to speak on your topic; it is not to provide an exhaustive resumé and so will be much shorter than your long bio. Your audience has come to hear you speak, not to hear someone speak about you, and an over-long introduction bio will mean they'll be bored before you've said a single word.

We recommend that the introduction bio not be any longer than 30 seconds. (Don't estimate this—read it out loud and time it.)

Here is an example of Matty's introduction bio for a speaking engagement on podcasting for authors, excerpted from her long bio (~100 words):

Matty Dalrymple (DAL-rim-ple) is the author of the Lizzy Ballard Thrillers and the Ann Kinnear (kin-NEAR) Suspense Novels and Suspense Shorts. She also podcasts, writes, speaks, and consults on the writing craft and the publishing voyage as The Indy Author. Since 2016 she has hosted hundreds of episodes of THE INDY AUTHOR PODCAST, and she is the author of books on podcasting for authors, on becoming an author speaker, and on creating income and connecting with readers using short fiction. Her articles have appeared in *Writer's Digest* magazine. She serves as the Campaigns Manager for the Alliance of Independent Authors.

She modifies the introduction bio based on the event. For example, if she is giving a talk on short fiction, she expands that portion to include the full title of the book and the fact that she co-authored it with Mark Leslie Lefebvre.

If rather than having someone else introduce you, you introduce yourself, don't read your introduction! You should have in mind the few points you want to hit (e.g., *fiction series names ... podcasts, writes, speaks, and consults as The Indy Author ... non-fiction books*). If you realize later in the talk that you forgot something, just mention it then.

The Cocktail Party Bio & The Guest Close-out

Although obviously not part of your official speaker package, there are two other types of bios you should have mentally ready to deliver smoothly.

One is the **cocktail party bio**—a very brief bio you use to introduce yourself in author / speaker social settings. For example:

Hi, I'm Matty Dalrymple! I write suspense, mystery, and thriller novels in the Ann Kinnear and Lizzy Ballard series, and I also have a non-fiction platform, The Indy Author, focused on the writing craft and the publishing voyage.

Note that the part of Matty's bios that addresses her non-fiction platform always references "the writing craft and the publishing voyage" in order to embed this branding verbiage in the listeners' mind and subtly convey her use of nautical metaphors for these topics.

Although not exactly a bio, we include the **guest close-out** in this section because it, like the cocktail party bio, is another good bit of verbiage to practice enough that you can deliver it smoothly. This is the information you share when, at the end of a podcast interview, for example, the host asks you to let listeners and viewers know where they can find out more about you online.

Don't list every place your audience members can find you! That will end what will no doubt be an informative and entertaining guest gig with a boring recitation of URLs and social media handles. Instead, send members to one place—probably your website—and ensure they can reach all your other platforms from there. For example, Matty's guest close-out is:

You can find out more about the Ann Kinnear Suspense Novels and Suspense Shorts and the Lizzy Ballard Thrillers at MattyDalrymple.com, and you can find out more about my non-fiction platform, where I explore the writing craft and the publishing voyage, at TheIndyAuthor.com. And I'd love to connect with listeners on Facebook at Matty Dalrymple and The Indy Author.

Note that the construction of the closing means that listeners hear Matty's name and brand a couple of times, embedding it in their memory, but without it sounding forced or awkward.

General Topic Information

Provide an online source of information on the topics on which you are qualified to speak. If your talks are focused on one area, create a web page related to that. If you offer talks on multiple areas, have one page that provides a list of topics, with a high-level description of each and, as appropriate, links to more detail on a page dedicated to each topic.

Upcoming and Past Events

Organizers often want to look over a list of your past events when they are considering you for a speaking engagement, and after attendees of an event have heard you speak once, they will want to know where you'll be speaking in the future! It's handy for both these audiences to have a central, basic list of your events available. Make sure the URL is easy to remember and easy to say; for example, Matty's events page is MattyDalrymple.com/Events.

Event-specific Web Page

This resource is one that will be focused on participants and provides information on a particular talk.

If the organizer allows it, use this page to post a downloadable copy of your presentation. If you include the URL and a QR code linking to the website page on the first slide of your presentation, attendees will be incentivized to access the page and will then be presented with the information you include there, so it can be a great way to, for example, get sign-ups to your email newsletter if you include a sign-up form.

The URL should be easy to remember and easy to say, since you will no doubt be referencing it in your talk as well as including it in any handouts. It should reference the event name—for example, authorlevelup.com/SelfPubCon.

Within the parameters of what the organizer allows you to share, the page should:

- Visually tie to your talk (for example, use the same colors and aesthetic as your slides)
- Be easy to navigate at a glance – Use big buttons

and images to highlight the items you want visitors to the page to find.
- Include anything you promised to give away in your talk such as a free book, supplemental materials, bibliographies, links, or resource recommendations.
- If you are giving away PDFs or checklists, host them on your site and share the URLs.
- If you are giving away a free ebook, use a service like BookFunnel or StoryOrigin to deliver it to participants and handle any support issues.
- Include book covers and links to books you want to promote.
- Provide a form to sign up for your email newsletter.
- Provide a link to your calendar if you do consultations.
- If possible, for in-person events, include a photo of yourself at the venue in front of a recognizable landmark – Put that image at the top of the page with a caption, "Hey, <Event Name> attendees!" This builds rapport with event attendees and ensures that they recognize you at the event.

An effective event-specific web page builds your audience before the event, provides invaluable resources to attendees during and after your talk, and can attract followers who will find you long after the event is a distant memory.

Headshot

A headshot is the photograph of you that you and event organizers will use to promote your talk. It might be the first exposure event attendees have to you, so it needs to reflect your topic and connect with your target audience.

As the name suggests, a headshot is usually a tightly cropped photo of your head, neck, and shoulders. This tight cropping is important because headshots are often presented at a small size, and you want viewers of your headshot to be able to recognize you in person at the venue.

An effective headshot is an important part of your speaker toolkit, but you can use it in many other places—for example, as your social media profile picture, on the About page on your website, and even on the back covers of your books. It is a key part of your branding, so invest some time and careful thought, and be willing to invest some money, to make sure that it supports your brand.

Establishing Your Audience-Facing Persona

What persona do you want to convey with your headshot? If your topic is lessons learned as a Fortune 500 executive and your target audience is fellow C-level executives, then a studio headshot in formal business attire is appropriate. If your topic is opportunities available in the restaurant industry for recent college graduates, then a more informal pose, perhaps with a restaurant background, is appropriate. If you're giving a talk on achieving ambitious goals, then a photo of you standing at the northern terminus of the Appalachian Trail after a solo through hike would set exactly the right tone.

Accommodating Multiple Personas

Do you have different platforms that require different personas? You may want different headshots for each.

For example, Matty uses a different headshot for appearances focused on her Matty Dalrymple fiction work than for appearances focused on The Indy Author non-fiction work. The aesthetic is consistent across the photos: casual poses and casual clothing in outdoor settings. However, the details vary: darker clothing and a more serious expression for the fiction persona than the non-fiction persona.

Similarly, for Michael's fiction persona, he uses a more relaxed, three-quarter pose, while for his non-fiction persona, he uses a slightly more formal pose, sitting forward and looking directly at the camera. However, the overall look is consistent, with the same clothing and same brick wall background.

You might even consider adjusting your headshot based on the event and venue. Although consistency is generally one of the keys to the success of a personal brand, of which your headshot is an important part, it can be fun to modify the background of your headshot to match the venue of the event. For a speaking engagement near Boston, Matty used a simple photo editing app to remove the background of her headshot and replace it with a royalty-free image of the Boston skyline. The goal was not to fool people into thinking the photo was taken in Boston, but to incorporate a lighthearted acknowledgement of the venue's location.

One thing we do not recommend is using extreme or unusual framing for your official headshot—for example, an extreme close-up of just your features, or with your face partially obscured or out-of-frame. As with the Boston example, this might be fine for a specific application. For example, Matty knows a group of mystery authors whose blog posts are accompanied by headshots of the authors with their faces partially obscured: one peers at the camera over a book, another has a fedora pulled low over her face. These headshots are fun and appropriate to the context, but all these authors have other, more conventionally composed shots as their official headshots.

The issue with oddly composed headshots is that, especially for events, your photo will appear with those of other speakers, and organizers generally want a consistent look. Plus, a photo of you holding a book in front of your face will defeat one of the primary goals of an event headshot: enabling other event attendees to recognize you.

It's best for your official headshot to include your head, neck, and shoulders in their entirety. Organizers may want to digitally remove the background and place it against an alternate background, and a very tightly cropped headshot might result in an unnatural-looking border.

When naming your headshot image, don't call it *Headshot* —imagine the irritation of the event organizer who has to sort through dozens of speaker headshots all called *Headshot*. Include not only your name but also a reference to the orientation and cropping—e.g., *Matty Dalrymple Headshot Portrait Tight Crop.jpg* or *Matty Dalrymple Headshot Landscape Wide Shot.jpg*.

Levels of Professionalism

One of our key themes throughout this book is that professionalism is everything, and here we consider some questions you might have about the level of professionalism required for your headshot.

Can I use a selfie?

If you reach the terminus of the Appalachian Trail at the end of your hike and find no one there to snap your photo, a selfie is completely acceptable. In fact, it might be the best option for representing the solo nature of the effort.

However, this example is a rare exception to what we recommend as a best practice regarding headshots: no selfies.

Selfies are fine for social media ("Here I am at the beach!" "Here I am walking my dog!"), but they are not professional, and professionalism is what event organizers and your audience expect from you as a speaker. You wouldn't want to go to a fine dining restaurant and have your gourmet meal served to you on plastic dinnerware. You want your speaker brand to be consistently professional, and a selfie does not convey professionalism.

Can I at least use a mobile phone camera?

Mobile phone cameras offer functionality that used to be found only in DSLR (digital single lens reflex) cameras, including auto focus, high resolution, and light correction. However, there are some effects that are harder to achieve with a mobile phone camera, such as shallow depth of field (blurry backgrounds). You may be able to mimic such an effect by using photo editing software to remove the background of your headshot and replace it with one more to your liking, but the effect may look artificial.

Results using a mobile phone can be fine, especially if you're on a budget, but they will never match the results of a professional-grade camera ... especially one wielded by a professional photographer.

But professional photographers are expensive! Can I ask a friend to take my photo?

There are undoubtedly advantages to having a friend take your photo, and not just lower cost. Having a friend rather than a photography pro behind the camera might make it easier for you to relax, a key requirement for an attractive headshot.

However, unless your friend is a professional photographer, they may not be equipped to optimize all the components of the photo, like what effect different backgrounds will have and the overall composition of the photo. If money is tight, having a friend take your photo is better than using a selfie, but you will get the most professional results if you go to a pro.

Hiring a Professional

Consider the benefits of hiring a professional photographer:

- They come armed with a professional-grade camera and a host of other equipment such as special lenses, reflectors, and strobes that will ensure your headshot is of the highest quality.
- They know exactly which camera settings to use for every situation.
- They have an intuitive sense for choosing the right location for your headshot and have the experience to suggest locations you would never think of. For example, Matty's photographer knew of a Blair Witch-esque hut made of branches and twigs in the park where they were shooting Matty's headshots—a background that was perfect for an author of suspense, mystery, and thrillers.
- They know how to position you to take best advantage of the setting—for example, posing you under a tree so that the light filtering through the branches highlights your face while keeping your shoulders in shadow.
- They can use photo manipulation software to edit out blemishes so that you look your best.

If we've convinced you that hiring a pro is the way to go, you no doubt have some more questions.

How can I make hiring a professional photographer affordable?

As with any profession, the fees professional photographers charge vary dramatically, so it pays to shop around. If cost is a consideration (and when is it not?), here are some ideas to make hiring a pro affordable.

- If you're having family photos done, pay the photographer a little extra to take some headshots of just you.
- Poll your local writer's group asking if others need headshots taken or updated, then approach photographers with the offer of providing them with several clients at once. Since the photographer will benefit from the efficiency of the gig, they may be willing to provide a discount (not charge the same fee that they would for taking photos of all the participants individually). However, since there will be some set-up time for each subject, you shouldn't expect them to charge the same as they would for one person. Finding a happy medium ground will benefit you and the photographer.
- Anything that saves you and the photographer time will save you money. If you need multiple headshots for multiple personas, as Matty does for her Matty Dalrymple fiction platform and The Indy Author non-fiction platform, consider accommodating this through a change of clothes and accessories rather than a change of location.

What should I consider when hiring and working with a professional photographer?

Here are some things to think about:

- Everyone knows someone who knows someone who is a photographer. Start within your network.

You should be able to find someone by word of mouth. A simple post on social media will help you get the process started. If you must, you can also do a web search for photographers in your area. Ask around for reviews or look at online postings about that photographer to gauge their professionalism.

- Get at least three quotes. To make sure you're comparing equivalent quotes, specify what should be included. Professional photographers will generally provide a flat fee that covers the pre-shoot consultation, their travel to and from the shoot location, their time at the shoot (including time you take to change outfits, for example), a digital contact sheet of raw shots (usually at least a few dozen for you to choose from), and retouching of your chosen photos (such as color balancing and removing blemishes). Make sure you tell them how many final photographs you want—for example, a serious version and a smiling version for a fiction and a non-fiction platform. Shop around to get the best deal.
- Once you have selected your photographer, get in writing an agreement on the services and deliverables to be provided. Matty was grateful to have a signed addendum to the agreement for her wedding photos specifying that she did not plan to purchase an album, especially when the photographer forgot about that agreement.
- Tap into your photographer's creative as well as technical expertise. Let them know what kind of persona you want to convey in your photos; they can make suggestions for clothing and venue.

How often do I need to update my headshot?

It's disappointing to get to know your favorite authors through their headshots and then meet them in person and find they look nothing like their photos. To avoid disappointing event attendees in this way, consider updating your headshot every two to three years, or more often if your appearance changes significantly, perhaps because of a new hairstyle or weight gain or loss. This schedule also avoids your headshot reflecting an outdated hairstyle or clothing. We recommend not using a heavily retouched photo because this, too, creates a distracting disconnect between your headshot and reality.

I hate having my picture taken! Do I have to have a headshot?

Yes, you have to have a headshot. If you're willing to stand on an actual or virtual stage in front of an audience—as you no doubt are if you are reading this book—then having your photograph taken should be a fraction as stressful! Any self-consciousness you have about your appearance in photographs provides an even stronger justification for hiring a professional photographer who knows all the tricks to relax you during the shoot, pose you in a flattering way, and process the photographs to highlight your best features.

What can I do to make my headshot the best it can be?

The best headshots are those where the subject looks comfortable and at ease, and the best way to achieve this is to *be* comfortable and at ease. Choose a location where you can relax. Matty avoids locations where there are likely to be passersby. Avoid distractions. If you're having the photos taken in your home, ask a friend to host your children at their house during the shoot.

The photographer as well as the surroundings will influence your ability to relax. When you're assessing photographers, consult not only the numbers in their quotes but also your gut—you're not likely to look relaxed if you dislike the person behind the camera.

Tell them what will help you relax. For example, Matty asks her photographers to count down to the moment they snap the photo ("three ... two ... one ..." *click*) so that she can smile on "one" rather than trying to hold a smile until her cheek muscles spasm.

And despite any advice we have offered earlier in this section, choose clothes, hair, and makeup that makes you feel attractive, because knowing you're going to look great in your headshot is the best way to achieve a great-looking headshot.

Business Cards

In this era of sharing information electronically, business cards might seem like a thing of the past, but they still have their place, especially at speaking events. Some might say, "But they just get thrown away!" We'll share advice for how to make sure your cards are not the ones that are merely discarded.

In this section, we will address the power of business cards, design tips for your cards, and how you can promote connections as a recipient of someone else's business card.

The Power of the Card

A business card is an almost instant means of sharing your contact information with another person—no need to get out your phone or fumble with an app. To capitalize on this benefit, you need to be able to get to your cards quickly. Michael keeps his cards in his shirt pocket. Matty has found that the holders that many event organizers provide for attendees' name tags is a great place to carry a few easily accessible cards.

They represent you even when you're not present. Be sure to leave a supply of cards on a table in the room where you are speaking for attendees to pick up. This is especially important at multi-talk events because attendees of your talk might want to speak with you afterwards but not be able to because the room must be cleared for the next talk, or they have to get to the next talk. Many conferences set aside a table in a public area for just this purpose, so make sure your cards are there as well. (Some conference organizers explicitly ask attendees *not* to leave their cards around the venue, so of course comply with their request.)

Use your card as a conversation starter by using an attention-getting, brand-appropriate design. You might use a striking photo or incorporate elegant elements like foil stamping. If a recipient exclaims about the unique nature of your card, it can be an entrée to an actual conversation!

Design Tips

- Use both sides of the card. If you have two brands, you might use one side for each, as long as they're compatible. For example, Matty's cards feature her fiction platform on one side and her non-fiction platform, The Indy Author, on the other.
- Make at least one side of your business card light-colored and non-glossy. This way, others can use it to jot notes about their interaction with you should they wish. (Pen ink tends to smear on glossy cards.)
- Don't clutter the card. Don't cram so much information onto the card that the text is difficult

to read. Consider using a QR code to enable the recipient to find that additional detail online.
- Include a photo of yourself on the card. How many times have we interacted with dozens of people at a conference, gotten home with a stack of business cards, then had no memory of who we got the cards from? A photo will be an instant reminder for the recipient about your interaction.
- Include your phone number. "What?" you might say (as Matty did when Michael made that recommendation). In the many years during which Michael has had his phone number on his cards, he has received just a few phone calls (not the hundreds of spam calls one might expect) and one of those resulted in a speaking engagement. Make it easy for the people who want to engage with you to do so. Most people are terrified at the thought of calling someone these days, so most won't take you up on the opportunity. When they do, interesting things could happen.

Michael once received a phone call on a Saturday morning. The caller introduced himself as the president of a prominent publishing organization in the United States. He also happened to be the organizer for an upcoming event that his organization was sponsoring, and he wanted to know if Michael was available to speak. Michael checked his calendar, immediately said yes, and came up with a pitch for a session on the spot, which the organizer accepted. Five minutes later, all the details were ironed out, and Michael had a paid speaking gig—an opportunity that might not have come about if he had not been easy to reach by phone.

- Consider the longevity of the information. Review your business cards periodically for outdated information, especially if you have a big supply of cards. Order new ones if anything on the card is out of date.

It's possible to get business cards made very inexpensively, but as with every presentation of yourself and your work, consider what brand you want to convey. One of Matty's guests on The Indy Author Podcast, in a discussion of marketing lessons authors can learn from other industries, mentioned the beautiful cards offered by tattoo artists at a convention he attended. This is an industry that is all about creating striking visuals, and it's vital that every representation of their work—including their business cards—be visually striking.

In fact, consider ways you can move beyond the traditional idea of *business cards*. For example, are you speaking on a sports-related topic? Consider getting cards that mimic sports trading cards.

Make them multi-functional. Matty got her business cards printed in portrait orientation and uses them as bookmarks when signing or sending out a book.

However, there is such a thing as going overboard and being gimmicky. Never forget what a business card is meant to do: convey your contact information to other people.

If you feel uncomfortable designing your own cards, many websites offer predesigned templates. You just need to select the design that best matches your brand and personal aesthetic.

Promoting Connection as a Card Recipient

The exchange of business cards is a two-way interaction,

and we have some tips to make the most of the ones you receive.

If you take a selfie with someone you just met, take a photo of their business card immediately afterwards so you can identify them later.

After your interaction, jot a few quick notes on the card about the person and your conversation. In case the person has not heeded the advice about the downside of double-sided glossy cards, have a pad of small sticky notes you can affix to the card for these notes.

Make sure you have a place to quickly store cards you receive from others. Those same event-provided name tag holders that Matty uses for her supply of her own business cards often include auxiliary pockets that are perfect for that purpose.

There are of course more high-tech alternatives to physical business cards—cards or apps that transfer your contact information to another person's Contact list with the tap of a phone or scan of a code—but as with all technology, this is changing so rapidly that any information we included on these options would quickly be outdated. Just search online for *best electronic business cards* and the current year to explore options. This is a great option to have available—for one thing, it's easy to update the information on the fly—but we still believe in the value of being able to hand someone a well-designed physical card.

Demo Reel

When pitching yourself as a speaker, it's convenient to point organizers to a central online location where they will find examples of you speaking on your proposed topic. For example, Matty has separate pages on her website where she provides links to or embeds examples of her speaking on a specific topic—becoming an author speaker, podcasting for authors, short fiction, story framing—on podcasts, webinars, and other venues.

But what if you're just starting out on your speaking career and you don't yet have these examples to share? Create your own demo reel.

To produce the components of a demo reel, you want to create an environment that mimics as much as possible the venues you want to pitch. Are you pitching in-person events? Style your space to resemble a stage. Are you pitching virtual events? Make sure your audio and video reflect the level of professionalism you will deliver in an actual event. Interested in interview formats? Enlist a friend or colleague to interview you. (You can even provide the questions.)

The goal is not to fool the event organizer into thinking this is an actual event but to demonstrate your expertise in your proposed topic and your skill in and comfort with discussing it. The level of professionalism demonstrated by a well-produced demo reel will illustrate to the organizer that you will be an easy person to work with.

Here are simple steps to creating your demo reel:

- Treat the shooting of your demo reel like a virtual presentation. Film it with the same energy and focus you'd use if you were filming a real presentation. Choose your background and props wisely, dress for the events you want to obtain, and be fastidious about every detail prospective organizers see.
- Prepare an introduction for yourself as well as two minutes of material that you would present in a virtual talk. Keep it to one impactful slide. You

should cover a golden nugget that gives the audience value and demonstrates your expertise as a speaker. Use a scaled-down version of the techniques we cover in the section on "Slides" to prepare the slide.
- Deliver two minutes' worth of material and demonstrate your expertise. Don't be afraid to shoot multiple takes. End the video with a call to action on where organizers can contact you.
- You don't have to pay for video editing software. Use free software like Movie Maker (Windows) or iMovie (Mac) to edit the video into its final form. There are many tutorials on how to use them on YouTube, so the learning curve should be shallow. If you're uncomfortable doing this, use an online marketplace to find someone who can do an inexpensive edit for you.
- Export your video and upload it to your site. It will serve as a compelling example of your speaking ability.
- Update your demo reel as needed. As you land actual events, consider creating a better demo reel with actual footage from your events, as allowed by the organizers, to further improve your credibility.

Speaker's Notes

Capture your responses to the questions below in the downloadable document available at https://www.theindyauthor.com/from-page-to-platform.html.

- How many of the components of a speaker toolkit do you already have, and what refinements might you want to make to them based on the advice in this section?
- Which components of a speaker toolkit do you need to create, and in what order will you prioritize their creation?
- What might you use as the topic of your demo reel?

STAYING AT THE CUTTING EDGE OF YOUR NICHE

Retaining your status as a professional author speaker is an ongoing process; you need to be both an expert in and a student of your topic area. Staying on top of news and developments enables you to incorporate these into your talks and presentation materials as appropriate and ensures that you continue to provide top-notch quality to your audiences year after year. This section includes our recommendations for how to do that.

Study. Read extensively in the source material in your topic area. If you are a lawyer, read the relevant cases in your niche—both those that your audience will most likely be familiar with as well as less familiar cases. If you want to speak on writing space operas, then you must have read extensively in that genre to be familiar with the plots, the tropes, and the most popular practitioners.

Stay up to date on what other experts in your topic area are saying. If another eminent expert in your field gave a talk on YouTube, watch it. If there's a new article about your niche, read it. Subscribe to the sources that track activity in your niche. Keep a notebook—actual or electronic—of emerging trends or unique angles. (Electronic has the advantage of being more easily searchable.)

Share. You can gain added benefit by sharing what you learn. Discuss it on your blog or share it on social media (and flag the creator). It's one thing to consume all the relevant content in your niche; it's another thing to contextualize it. Speakers who do this often generate leads because they offer compelling takes that get people thinking. This is great marketing.

Experiment. Keep an eye out for opportunity and make leaps and strides forward in your area of expertise by experimenting. For example, Michael is a global expert on dictation and transcription. He has done things with dictation that very few have even considered, and his unique approach to this popular but unusual writing method is head-turning. Michael continues to develop his unique dictation style, and he regularly works with programmers to refine the approach. He talks about this frequently on his platform, and his experiments are great material for a talk because they are unusual.

Build Your Network. A speaker is only as strong as their network. If you are an expert in your niche but don't know other experts in your niche on a first-name basis, you're doing it wrong. Matty has developed a world-class network by interviewing an incredible range of speakers, entrepreneurs, and creatives on The Indy Author Podcast. Michael has an extensive network of contacts through his work on YouTube and the Alliance of Independent Authors.

Building your network gives you a pool of fellow experts with whom you can exchange ideas. Mentioning members of your network in your talk (without being obnoxious about it) emphasizes your credibility and deepens the rapport with your audience because they will see you as "connected." It also illustrates your willingness as a professional to learn from others—even though we are experts in our niches, we can't know *everything*. Audiences respect the speaker who has an impressive network and knows how to use it to further their expertise.

You *must* stay at the cutting edge of your niche. Yes, it takes time and effort, but it makes for more compelling talks. It also shows the audience that you are truly an expert. It shows organizers that you put time and thought into your material. And most importantly, it will lead to more opportunities for you down the road.

Speaker's Notes

Capture your responses to the questions below in the downloadable document available at https://www.theindyauthor.com/from-page-to-platform.html.

- What steps will you take to ensure you stay at the cutting edge of your niche?

AFTERWORD

There is so much to learn as a speaker. We consider ourselves experienced professional speakers, and we are always learning new things. Every experience adds to your pool of speaker wisdom: the wisdom to know how to help out an organizer who is in the weeds, to deal with hecklers gracefully, to improvise when the venue's computer dies, or the virtual meeting platform misbehaves, or you experience a wardrobe malfunction on stage or on camera.

But wisdom not only means dealing with the bad but capitalizing on the good. It's having the experience to know which organizers will be easiest to work with and whose engagements will be the most fulfilling. It means being able to pitch yourself to those organizers successfully, event after event. It's packing a room with people eager to hear you share your knowledge and then having them become your most devoted fans. It's being so comfortable with the entire process that you can predict what the organizer is going to ask for before they ask for it and address your audience's questions before they raise them.

It means having all the tools and knowledge and gaining

AFTERWORD

all the career and personal benefits of being a true professional.

In fact, you might agree with us that it's a lot like the wisdom you gain as you develop professionalism as a writer.

We hope that our advice paves the way for a successful transition from page to platform—drop us a note and let us know how it's going!

Matty@MattyDalrymple.com

Michael@MichaelLaRonn.com

Speaker's Notes

Review the information you captured in the downloadable Speaker's Notes document (available at https://www.theindyauthor.com/from-page-to-platform.html) and make any adjustments needed to reflect your evolving understanding of your goals and plans for your career as an author speaker.

ABOUT THE AUTHORS

Matty Dalrymple is the author of the Lizzy Ballard Thrillers and the Ann Kinnear Suspense Novels and Suspense Shorts. She also podcasts, writes, speaks, and consults on the writing craft and the publishing voyage as The Indy Author. Writer's Digest has including TheIndyAuthor.com on its list of 101 Best Websites for Writers for multiple years. Since 2016 she has hosted hundreds of episodes of The Indy Author Podcast. She is the author of nonfiction books for authors and her articles have appeared in *Writer's Digest* magazine and *Indie Author Magazine*. She serves as the Campaigns Manager for the Alliance of Independent Authors. You can find Matty's fiction at https://www.mattydalrymple.com/ and her resources for writers at https://www.theindyauthor.com/.

Michael La Ronn is the author of over 100 science fiction & fantasy books and self-help books for writers. He writes from the great plains of Iowa and has managed to write while raising a family, working a full-time job, and even attending law school classes in the evenings. Michael also runs the award-winning YouTube channel "Author Level Up," with over 50,000 subscribers and 2 million views. *Writer's Digest* voted the channel one of the "Best Resources for Writers" in 2020. You can find his fiction at www.michaellaronn.com and his videos and books for writers at www.authorlevelup.com.

ALSO BY MATTY DALRYMPLE

The Lizzy Ballard Thrillers

Rock Paper Scissors (Book 1)

Snakes and Ladders (Book 2)

The Iron Ring (Book 3)

Kill Box Checkmate (Book 3½)

Scare Card (Book 4)

Drawing Dead (Book 5)

The Lizzy Ballard Thrillers Ebook Box Set

The Ann Kinnear Suspense Novels

The Sense of Death (Book 1)

The Sense of Reckoning (Book 2)

The Falcon and the Owl (Book 3)

A Furnace for Your Foe (Book 4)

A Serpent's Tooth (Book 5)

Be with the Dead (Book 6)

The Ann Kinnear Suspense Novels Ebook Box Set - Books 1-3

The Ann Kinnear Suspense Shorts

All Deaths Endure

Close These Eyes

May Violets Spring

Ministers of Grace

Our Dancing Days

Sea of Troubles

Stage of Fools

Write in Water

Non-Fiction

Taking the Short Tack: Creating Income and Connecting with Readers Using Short Fiction with Mark Leslie Lefebvre

The Indy Author's Guide to Podcasting for Authors: Creating Connections, Community, and Income

From Page to Platform: How to Succeed as an Author Speaker with M.L. Ronn

Collaborate to Create: A Guide to Coauthoring Nonfiction with M.L. Ronn

The Podcast Guest Playbook: Turning Conversations into Connections and Community with Mark Leslie Lefebvre

Copyright 2024 © William Kingsfield Publishers and M.L. Ronn. All rights reserved.

Published by William Kingsfield Publishers

Cover design by Matty Dalrymple

Cover image by Quils via Deposit Photos

No part of this book may be reproduced or used in any manner without written permission of the author except for the use of quotations in a book review.

Authors reserve the rights, and no one has the rights to reproduce and/or otherwise use this work in any manner for purposes of training artificial intelligence technologies to generate text, including without limitation, technologies that are capable of generating works in the same style or genre as the work without the Authors' specific and express permission to do so.

ISBN-13: 978-1-959882-15-2 (Print)

www.ingramcontent.com/pod-product-compliance
Lightning Source LLC
Chambersburg PA
CBHW062200080426
42734CB00010B/1759